DISCARD

Pioneers

THE LEAKEYS

rourke biographies

Pioneers

THE LEAKEYS

by
LISA A. LAMBERT

Rourke Publications, Inc.
Vero Beach, Florida 32964

∞ The paper used in this book conforms to the American National Standard for Permanence of Paper for Printed Library Materials, Z39.48-1984.

Library of Congress Cataloging-in-Publication Data
Lambert, Lisa Ann, 1958-
   The Leakeys / written by Lisa A. Lambert.
     p. cm. — (Rourke biographies. Pioneers)
   Includes bibliographical references and index.
   Summary: Highlights the accomplishments of the family of paleoanthropologists which made important fossil discoveries in Africa.
   ISBN 0-86625-492-7 (alk. paper)
   1. Leakey, L. S. B. (Louis Seymour Bazett), 1903-1972—Juvenile literature. 2. Leakey family—Juvenile literature. 3. Anthropologists—Kenya—Biography—Juvenile literature.   4. Fossil man—Africa, East—Juvenile literature. [1. Leakey, L. S. B. (Louis Seymour Bazett), 1903-1972. 2. Leakey family. 3. Anthropologists. 4. Fossil man.] I. Title. II. Series.
GN21.L368L35   1993
301'.092'2—dc20
[B]   92-46046
                                              CIP
                                              AC

PRINTED IN THE UNITED STATES OF AMERICA

Contents

Chapter 1.   The White African 11
Chapter 2.   A Family Affair 20
Chapter 3.   A Partnership Is Formed 28
Chapter 4.   The Glory Years 36
Chapter 5.   Footprints in the Past 46
Chapter 6.   The Second Generation 70
Chapter 7.   The Bones of Lake Turkana 78
Chapter 8.   The Leakey Legacy 87

Time Line 97
Important Discoveries 100
Glossary 102
Bibliography 104
Media Resources 107
Index 109

Color Illustrations

1. Louis Leakey
2. Olduvai Gorge, Tanzania
3. *Zinjanthropus* memorial
4. Louis and Richard Leakey at Omo Valley
5. *Zinjanthropus*
6. Louis and Mary Leakey with *Zinjanthropus*
7. Tanzania
8. Richard Leakey with *Homo erectus* skull
9. Richard Leakey near Koobi Fora
10. Richard Leakey at Lake Turkana
11. Richard and Mary Leakey
12. Richard Leakey with Meave
13. The Museum at Olduvai
14. Richard Leakey in Nairobi

THE LEAKEYS

Chapter 1

The White African

Chief Koinange of the Kikuyu people of eastern Africa once said the following about Louis Leakey: "We call him the Black man with a white face, because he is more of an African than a European, and we regard him as one of ourselves." Louis Leakey always loved Africa and its peoples. This love led him back to Africa again and again, searching for fossils. Leakey's love of Africa and fossils was shared by his second wife, Mary. It was also shared by the Leakey children, especially Richard.

Child in the Wild

Louis Seymour Bazett Leakey was born on August 7, 1903, in Kabete, Kenya. Kabete was a small village of mud and thatched huts, which could be reached only on foot. Louis' father and mother were English missionaries, sent by the Church Missionary Society to work with the Kikuyu people of eastern Africa. Louis, his sisters Julia and Gladys, and his brother Douglas spent most of their childhood among the Kikuyu.

With the other boys his age, Louis learned all the skills and customs of the Kikuyu. He learned to speak the Kikuyu language like a native. He learned to hunt with a spear and to set traps for live birds and mammals, which he then sold to zoos. He trapped some animals—such as jackals, mongooses, and genet cats—for their skins, which he would sell. He also learned to make hives from tree trunks and to keep bees. When Louis was thirteen years old, his friends began to build their own bachelor quarters.

Louis used some of the money he had earned to buy materials for a house of his own. He built several huts, one with three rooms and walls lined with plaster. For the next three years, he worked and slept in his hut, although he still ate with his family in their house nearby.

Louis Leakey's interest in prehistory started when he was twelve. An English cousin sent him a Christmas present, a book called *Days Before History*. This book described the flint arrowheads and stone axes used by prehistoric people in Britain. The book inspired Louis to look for similar artifacts around his home. He actually found many arrowheads made of obsidian, a shiny black volcanic rock common in the area. Louis was helped by Arthur Loveridge, the assistant curator of the museum in Nairobi, eight miles away. Loveridge was a specialist in snakes, reptiles, and birds, but he taught Louis many of the important rules of collecting, including how to keep records of all the pieces he found.

Unlike his African friends, Louis and his sisters and brothers took lessons in Latin, French, and mathematics from a series of English governesses. The family also visited England several times, once for two years when Louis was three and again when Louis was seven. During World War I (1914-1918), Louis did not leave Africa again until it was time to begin his formal schooling. His relatively brief visits did little to prepare him for the very different life of British schools.

Life at School

Louis Leakey entered Weymouth College in January, 1920. He was sixteen and a half. Weymouth is an English "public school" (the equivalent of an American private high school). The customs and habits of the students there were as foreign to Louis as they would have been to any Kikuyu native. In his first autobiography, *White African* (1937), Leakey commented:

12

Louis Seymour Bazett Leakey. (AP/Wide World Photos)

I was being treated like a child of ten when I felt like a man of twenty, and it made me very bitter. I was not understood as an individual nor treated as such, and so I was not happy.

Despite his many difficulties, Louis Leakey finished the course at Weymouth in less than two years. In the summer of 1922, he took his exams for admission to the honors program of Cambridge University. Under the Cambridge tripos system, he could study anthropology only if he also chose a second area from among classical languages, modern languages, mathematics, science, or history. Of all of these disciplines, modern languages seemed the best bet, because he already knew how to speak and write French. Unfortunately, two languages were needed. After reviewing the rules, he proposed to the university authorities that for modern languages, he would study French and Kikuyu. Since Kikuyu was indeed a modern language, spoken by a large number of people, the university had to agree (although later the university would change the rules to prevent the choice of such "unusual" languages). Because no one at the university spoke Kikuyu, Louis tutored a professor in the language so that the professor could give Louis his exams.

Cambridge University is divided into many separate colleges. Originally, Louis had hoped to enter Peterhouse College, which his father had attended. Eventually, however, he chose to enter St. John's College, partly because of available financial aid and partly on the advice of one of his teachers at Weymouth. At St. John's he regained some of his precious freedom. He had private rooms, he could do his own cooking, and he could keep whatever hours he wished. His first year went very well, except that his poor showing in French literature prevented him from receiving a scholarship he wanted.

University life was not all work and no play. Despite Louis' dislike for cricket, he always enjoyed rugby (a popular British sport a bit like American football). In Kenya, he had organized the members of his age group into a team. At Weymouth, he had had some trouble adapting to the English rules of the game, and also to wearing shoes while playing. He still liked rugby, however, so he continued playing on a kind of junior varsity team while he was at St. John's. In October of his second year at St. John's, he suffered a concussion while on the field. Louis left school and spent ten days in the care of an aunt and uncle in Norfolk, England.

When Louis returned to school, he still suffered from severe headaches, and he even had a temporary loss of memory. His doctor ordered him to leave school for a year and to live someplace with plenty of fresh air. At first, this seemed like very bad news. Louis was poor and could not afford to live for a year without working. Eventually, however, a little bit of the Leakey luck came to his rescue. Through a friend of his family, Louis learned that the British Museum of Natural History was planning an expedition to look for dinosaur fossils in East Africa.

The expedition would look for sites in the interior of what was then Tanganyika. Tanganyika was at that time a British colony on the southern border of Kenya. After Tanganyika gained its independence, it joined with another former colony, Zanzibar, to form the modern nation of Tanzania. The leader of the expedition, W. E. Cutler, was an experienced archaeologist, but he had never been to Africa. The museum wanted someone who knew East Africa well, and who could serve as a coordinator, a travel adviser, and a translator. After a single interview, Louis got the job.

The First Expedition

Louis Leakey's first field trip to search for fossils was remarkable in many ways. Louis was only twenty years old; he had completed little more than one year of university training, and none of it was yet in anthropology. However, because of his childhood in Africa, Louis was an essential member of the

Louis and Mary painstakingly excavate pieces of bone at Olduvai Gorge in 1961. (AP/Wide World Photos)

team. While Cutler, the expedition's leader, waited in Tanganyika's capital, Dar-es-Salaam, for stores and equipment, Louis headed on to Lindi, the port nearest to the proposed camp site. In Lindi, Louis hired fifteen porters plus a cook, and then set off on safari into the interior. After several days they reached the site. Louis negotiated with the local people for workers and for daily supplies of food. With the help of the workers, he constructed a three-room house for Cutler and himself, with additional buildings and huts for more than one hundred native workers. He then proceeded to oversee the clearing of an

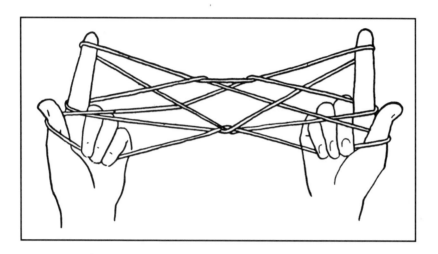

Making figures from pieces of string is a pastime popular with many African tribes. The Kikuyu are one of the few tribes that do not make such figures, so Louis Leakey did not learn to make them until he attended Cambridge University. Louis became very skilled with these figures and used them to make friends as he traveled through Africa. He once said that they might have saved his life: In 1929, he was traveling through Zambia and his truck broke down. Although many people passed, no one stopped to help. Louis pulled out his string and made a figure. A big crowd gathered. An old woman pulled out a string and made a figure of her own, which Louis copied. Soon, he had all the help he needed.

eight-foot-wide trail to allow boxes and heavy equipment to be transported. All this was done in eight short weeks, before the arrival of the expedition's leader.

W. E. Cutler was well known at that time as one of the best field collectors of fossil reptiles. While most of the digging was done by the hired workers, Cutler, with the help of Louis, identified the bones, extracted them from their sites, preserved them with shellac, and made casts of them with plaster of paris. Cutler also taught Louis much practical geology. Meanwhile, Louis continued supervising many of the housekeeping chores, including making crates for shipping the bones back to England and trapping many specimens of small mammals and birds for the museum.

Back to Cambridge

In January, 1925, Louis returned to Cambridge. His concussion still gave him problems occasionally, but he was able to continue his studies. To help support himself, he wrote and lectured about his field experience. His very first lecture was attended by a number of officials from the university and the British Museum, and Louis was very nervous. He even had to borrow the proper clothes to wear. Once he started talking, however, his fear disappeared. Later, Louis became a popular and experienced lecturer, but he wrote in *White African*:

> After this terrifying opening to my lecturing career the numerous lectures which I gave in various schools . . . were child's play, and I soon began to enjoy lecturing instead of hating it, but even now during the last few minutes before I actually start to speak I find myself seized with fear which is a kind of reflection of that awful first lecture at Cambridge.

The remaining years at Cambridge passed quickly and happily. Once Louis passed French literature, he was allowed to begin his studies of anthropology. From one professor, A. C. Haddon, he learned about string figures, knowledge which he later put to good use. Because of his earlier injury, Louis dropped rugby, but he played a lot of tennis. At one point, he was nearly dismissed from the college for daring to wear shorts to play tennis—an early example of Louis' impatience with established rules.

18

During these years, Louis published his first scientific paper, a scheme for classifying African bows and arrows. At the end of his school years, he was awarded first-place honors for his work in modern languages and anthropology. He was also rewarded with a six-year research fellowship from St. John's College.

Chapter 2

A Family Affair

In the introduction to one of his many books, Louis Leakey once wrote that "Where did I come from?" is a question asked by many children. "Where did human beings come from?" is the question asked by scientists like Louis and Mary Leakey and their son Richard. Through hard work, creative insight, and a large dose of luck, the members of the Leakey family have added a great deal to our knowledge of our human ancestors. At the same time, they have made the general public much more aware of the exciting developments in paleo-anthropology.

The Science of Fossils

The word "paleoanthropology" comes from combining three words of Greek origin. *Paleo* is a prefix meaning "ancient" or "long ago." *Anthrop* comes from the Greek word for human being, *anthropos*. Finally, the suffix *-ology* means "the study of." Putting them all together, paleoanthropology is the study of ancient human beings. In recent years, this definition has been extended to include the study of prehumans as well.

It is relatively easy to study people who lived, say, 500 years ago. For many cultures, we have written records that tell us what these people ate, what they did, and how long they lived. Still another source of information includes tools, such as stone axes, and other artifacts, such as cave paintings and bone carvings.

Such records are not available to study individuals who lived 50,000 or more years ago. For this reason, scientists rely on the study of fossils. Fossils are the remains of living creatures which have been preserved in rocks. Most of the time these remains are bones that were hardened by mineral deposits and buried in layers of rock. Fossils can also be the traces of living creatures: for example, a leaf pressed in the mud. Although the leaf will decay, its outline may be preserved in the dried mud for thousands of years. Footprints of early humans and prehumans also exist, preserved in the same way.

When a new fossil is found, especially a very old one, great care is taken to protect it. Fossils are sometimes buried in very hard rock that must be carefully chipped away. The exact location of a new fossil must be recorded. This is important in case other fossils are found nearby; the scientist wants to know if they are related in any way. Each fossil is assigned a number or code for later identification. Casts of each fossil may be made. The fossil is covered with a paste-like material that quickly hardens. When the cast is dry, it can be used as a mold to make copies of the fossil. These copies can then be studied or displayed in museums. Finally, each fossil is carefully packed for shipment to a laboratory where it can be thoroughly studied and where its age can be determined.

Humans and Prehumans

Through the study of fossils, scientists can learn many things. For example, by measuring the angle of the hip bones, one can tell if the individual was male or female. By looking at the way the leg bones join at the knee, a scientist can tell whether the individual walked upright or on all fours like a chimpanzee. Such studies can also reveal the diet, diseases, and age at death of a given individual.

With all the things that can be learned from a fossil, sometimes classifying it can be the most difficult part. In order to organize and better understand all living creatures and how

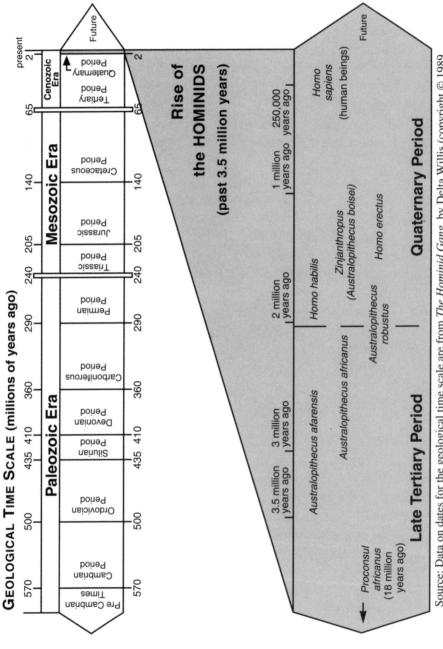

GEOLOGICAL TIME SCALE (millions of years ago)

Paleozoic Era

Pre Cambrian Times	Cambrian Period	Ordovician Period	Silurian Period	Devonian Period	Carboniferous Period	Permian Period
570	570 500	500	435 410	410 360	360 290	290 240

Mesozoic Era

Triassic Period	Jurassic Period	Cretaceous Period
240 205	205 140	140 65

Cenozoic Era

Tertiary Period	Quaternary Period
65 2	2 present

Future

Rise of the HOMINIDS
(past 3.5 million years)

Late Tertiary Period

Proconsul africanus (18 million years ago)

3.5 million years ago — Australopithecus afarensis

3 million years ago — Australopithecus africanus

2 million years ago — Homo habilis

Australopithecus robustus

Zinjanthropus (Australopithecus boisei)

Homo erectus

Quaternary Period

1 million years ago

250,000 years ago — Homo sapiens (human beings)

Future

Source: Data on dates for the geological time scale are from *The Hominid Gang*, by Delta Willis (copyright © 1989, Delta Willis), p. 288.

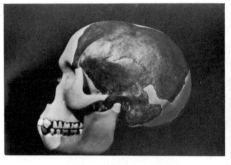
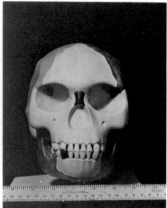

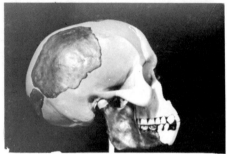

From F. Spencer, *The Piltdown Papers*. Natural History Museum Publications & Oxford University Press, 1990.
Reprinted by permission.

The Piltdown story is an embarrassing page in the history of paleoan-thropology. In 1912, an English lawyer and amateur archaeologist named Charles Dawson found some stone tools and an unusual fossil in a gravel bed near Piltdown Common, England. When the pieces of this skull were assembled, they appeared to show a creature with a large brain like a modern human, but with a very primitive jaw. In 1953, this "fossil" proved to be a fake: a human skull connected to the jaw of an ape. Many famous scientists were fooled by this hoax. Louis Leakey, however, never quite believed in "Piltdown man." Leakey thought that there must be an error, and in 1934 he wrote: "If the lower jaw really belongs to the same individual as the skull, then Piltdown man is unique in all humanity."

they are related, scientists use a special classification system. In this system, all living things are assigned to one of five kingdoms. Humans, for example, are members of the Animal Kingdom. Within each kingdom are other categories, called *phyla* (singular, *phylum*). Humans belong to the phylum Chordata (animals with a backbone). Other subdivisions include class (humans are in the class Mammalia), order (humans are Primates), and family (humans belong to the family Hominidae). Two further subdivisions, genus and species, are the most commonly used. Humans are given the scientific name *Homo sapiens*, meaning that human beings belong to the genus *Homo* and the species *sapiens*. The genus name can be abbreviated: *H. sapiens*.

There are no other living members of the genus *Homo*. However, many years ago, before *Homo sapiens*, the people who lived on the earth did not look quite like us. When scientists look at these older fossils, they can see differences between these fossils and modern human skeletons. Skulls that are around 400,000 years old held smaller brains than modern human skulls. Other differences include the lack of a prominent chin and the presence of bony ridges over the eyes. These and other changes led scientists to call individuals of this type *Homo erectus*, meaning that they belong to the same genus as we do, but to a different species. Going back 1.6 million years, still more differences can be seen. These even more primitive individuals are classified as *Homo habilis*.

Just as *Homo habilis* is an ancestor to modern humans, something else was an ancestor to *Homo habilis*. This "something else" was so primitive—so different—that it cannot be classified in the same species or even in the *Homo* genus. Instead, scientists use the term "hominid." This term refers to any member of the genus *Homo* but also includes the "pre-*Homo*" groups.

One of these "pre-*Homo*" hominid groups was the genus

Australopithecus. There are four commonly recognized species of *Australopithecus*. The oldest and most primitive is *A. afarensis*. There is some debate among scientists about whether this species coexisted with or changed into the next oldest species, *A. africanus*. Scientists also debate over which of these two species was the ancestor of the *Homo* line. The remaining two species, *A. boisei* and *A. robustus*, lived at the same time as *Homo habilis* and have no living descendants. All the species of *Australopithecus* are together called "australopithecines."

The earliest hominids had ape-like heads, possessed small brains, and walked upright. Exactly what sort of creature came before them in the line of human ancestors is a big question. At some point, humans and apes, members of the Primate order, all had a common ancestor. This ancestor probably lived around 18 million years ago, during the Miocene era. Several important fossil finds date from this period. Mary Leakey discovered the fossil remains of a creature named *Proconsul africanus*, which had features resembling both apes and monkeys. Another contender for the title of human ancestor is *Sivapithecus*, with its slightly more ape-like features. A smaller version, called *Ramapithecus*, lived about 14 million years ago, and it also has some claim as an ancestor to *Australopithecus*.

The "Leakey Luck"

Many of the most important fossil specimens of *Homo erectus* and *Homo habilis* were discovered by members of the Leakey family or members of their expeditions. Louis, his wife Mary, their son Richard, and Richard's wife Meave are the best-known members of the Leakey family. Louis identified (and named) the first *Homo habilis* skull. Mary and Louis, working together, found many important *Australopithecus* fossils. Mary, working alone after Louis died, found some

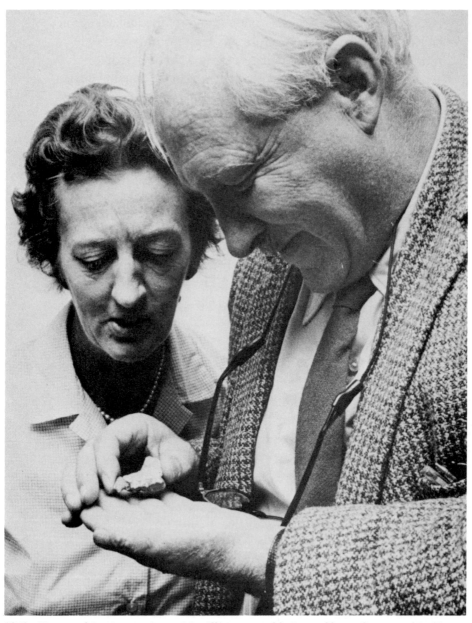

1962: Mary and Louis examine a 14-million-year-old piece of bone discovered in Kenya. (AP/Wide World Photos)

incredible fossil footprints of creatures who walked upright more than three and a half million years ago.

When Louis Leakey left on his first scientific expedition in 1926, he joined a science in its infancy. While many people had looked for and found fossils, little progress had been made in organizing and understanding the material. Louis and Mary had incredible good fortune in their years together, finding important examples of nearly every hominid and many pre-hominid species. Also, their partnership with the National Geographic Society and the resulting articles and television specials created widespread interest and support for the subject of paleoanthropology.

Louis died in 1972, and Mary's activities lessened after she lost her sight in one eye. However, their son Richard, curator of the Kenya National Museum, and his wife, Meave, have carried on the family tradition, including the typical "Leakey luck."

Chapter 3

A Partnership Is Formed

Louis and Mary Leakey were more than simply husband and wife; they were business partners, co-authors, colleagues, and parents. Together, they found uncountable numbers of fossils and artifacts, published numerous articles and books, and reared three sons. They faced many hardships together, but they never lost their love of prehistory or of Africa.

Louis: Early Expeditions

After graduating from Cambridge University in 1926, over the next five years Louis Leakey led three expeditions to Africa. The first trip included just Louis and an undergraduate assistant, Bernard H. Newsom, from Cambridge. The two of them lived in an old pigsty while they worked, and they managed to find more than thirty-eight Stone Age skeletons. The first and second expeditions both explored areas within a few hours' drive of Nairobi. Louis had an easy time getting supplies and was able to visit his family often. From information gathered during his first expedition, Louis wrote and submitted his first scientific paper, "Stone Age Man in Kenya Colony." It appeared in the British journal *Nature* on July 16, 1927. For the first time he worked at Olduvai Gorge, the site of some of his most famous discoveries. There, he and his coworkers found many fossils and artifacts and wrote a letter that involved him in his first controversy.

While on his first expedition, Louis had met a young woman named Henrietta Wilfrida Avern, who was visiting some nearby settlers. "Frida," as she was called, was a teacher, two years older than Louis. They liked each other immediately, and in 1928 they were married. In 1931, their first child was born, a daughter named Priscilla Muthoni. Louis chose for her middle name a Kikuyu word that is also used as a term of affection. Two years later, in 1933, their second child, Colin Louis, was born.

Louis and Frida had many things in common; they were both Cambridge graduates, and they were both intelligent, outspoken, and stubborn. Although they were very happy at first, eventually the marriage soured. Frida did not want to spend her whole life wandering from place to place, with no permanent home in which to rear her family. Louis did not want to be tied to one spot, waiting for his children to grow up. This unhappy situation might have continued for some time, but in 1933, Louis met Mary Douglas Nicol. Shortly after that, Louis and Frida separated, and they divorced in 1936. Louis and Mary were married on Christmas Eve, 1936.

Prehistory in Her Genes

Like Louis, Mary had a childhood that was a little bit odd. She was born on February 6, 1913, in London, England. Her father, Erskine Nicol, was a landscape painter, and the family traveled through Europe to allow him to find sites to paint. Each year they spent their winters in Italy, France, or Switzerland. In the summer, they returned to London, so that her father could sell his paintings. Mary's mother, Cecilia, was a member of the Frere family. Several of the Freres were interested in archaeology, including John Frere, the first discoverer of British Stone Age tools.

During her family's travels, Mary met some very famous people. Mary's father and mother had met in Egypt, and her father was always interested in Egyptology. He was a good friend of Howard Carter, one of the men who discovered the great tomb of Tutankhamen (popularly known as King Tut). Another close friend of the family was Abbé Lemozi, a priest

Mary Leakey presents the reconstructed skull of Zinjanthropus boisei *("Nutcracker Man")*
to Tanzania's President Julius Nyerere in 1965. (AP/Wide World Photos)

in the French village of Cabrerets. Abbé Lemozi was also a respected amateur archaeologist, and with him Mary studied stone tools and the cave paintings of France.

When Mary was only thirteen years old, her father died after a brief illness. She and her mother returned to England, and Mary attended school for the first time in her life. She had never before had formal schooling, and she did not adjust well to the restrictions of life at the different schools she briefly attended. At one school, she ate soap so that she would appear to be "foaming at the mouth," and on another occasion she deliberately caused an explosion in chemistry class. After expulsion from two schools, Mary was educated at home by her parents or tutors.

One summer, while Mary was in her teens, she and her mother visited Stonehenge, a great circle of giant stones made by prehistoric people. They visited a similar site at Avebury, and there she met Dorothy Liddell and her brother-in-law, Alexander Keiller, both famous archaeologists. Later, in her autobiography, *Disclosing the Past* (1984), Mary speculated that this visit might have first triggered the notion that a career in archaeology was possible for a woman.

As Mary grew older, her interest in archaeology also increased. With little formal schooling, however, she had no chance of being admitted to a university. She did attend some lectures in geology at London University and in archaeology at the London Museum. Mary also wanted experience working in the field, but without training, few people were willing to take her along. Finally, she persuaded Dorothy Liddell to take her on as an assistant. Mary worked with Liddell for three seasons at Hembury, one of the earliest Neolithic (late Stone Age) sites in Britain.

From her artist father, Mary had inherited a talent for drawing. As with archaeology, she had no formal training. She was able to combine her two interests by making drawings of

31

Jomo Kenyatta (left) was the first prime minister of Kenya and that nation's first president. He was also a Kikuyu, born Kamau Ngenegi. He later changed his name to Jomo (meaning "burning spear") Kenyatta (the Kikuyu name for a belt he wore). When Kenyatta was born, Kenya was a British colony. Kenyatta became active in a nationalist movement, the Kenyan African Union. In 1952, radical groups started the Mau Mau rebellion, and Kenyatta was arrested for allegedly being sympathetic to the rebels' cause. The paths of Kenyatta and the Leakeys crossed many times. Kenyatta's wife, Grace, was a former student of Louis' parents. Louis served as court interpreter at Kenyatta's trial. In 1966, while Kenyatta was president, he arranged for Louis to meet the emperor of Ethiopia, Haile Selassie. Through this meeting, Louis was able to persuade Haile Selassie to open his country to anthropologists.

many of the stone tools they found at Hembury. Some of these pictures were published and were admired by another woman archaeologist, Dr. Gertrude Caton-Thompson. She asked Mary to make drawings of stone tools she had found in Fayoum, Egypt.

In 1933, when Mary was twenty, Gertrude Caton-Thompson invited her to a lecture and dinner at the Royal Anthropological Institute in London. The speaker was Louis Leakey, who talked about his most recent trip to Africa. Mary and Louis sat next to each other at dinner and had a lively conversation. It was not love at first sight, but Louis was impressed with Mary's knowledge of archaeology and her ability to draw, and he asked her to help with the illustrations for his book, *Adam's Ancestors*. It was a partnership that would work equally well on other levels.

Louis Writes and Mary Digs

Shortly after their marriage, Louis was offered an unusual

33

job by members of the Rhodes Trust, a philanthropic organization. They wanted someone to record the ancient customs of the Kikuyu people before they were forgotten. The Rhodes Trust offered to pay Louis' salary for two years if he would take the project. Louis was reluctant to leave his fieldwork, but the project was an important one, and the money was more than welcome. Louis and Mary left for Kenya in January, 1937, shortly after their marriage. Louis met his old friend Chief Koinange, senior chief of all the Kikuyu. Koinange gave Louis the rank of first-grade elder and appointed a group of nine elders to act as advisers. At the end of the two years, Louis had enough information for a three-volume study on Kikuyu history, customs, and traditions.

While Louis gathered his information, Mary pursued paleoanthropology. She worked at a site called Hyrax Hill, just outside the town of Nakuru. Mary excavated and surveyed a number of Stone Age and Iron Age burial mounds and settlements that she found there. Her findings were not published until 1945, but her work on the site finally won her recognition as a professional archaeologist. The Kenyan government later declared Hyrax Hill an "ancient monument" and opened a museum at the site.

While working at Hyrax Hill, Mary made friends with many of the local settlers. One very close friend was Nellie Grant, who ran a nearby thousand-acre ranch. Nellie was the inspiration for "Tilly" in the book *The Flame Trees of Thika* (1974), written by Nellie's daughter, Elspeth Huxley. Nellie arranged for Mary to give her first public talk, a lecture on Hyrax Hill, before members of the Njoro Country Club.

World War II

Louis and Mary remained in Africa during World War II. Louis was hired by the Kenyan government to work in civil intelligence. His main task was to counteract the spread of anti-British propaganda. He earned additional money by selling medicines and other supplies to the Kikuyu. In 1940, Louis accepted a post as curator of the Coryndon Museum in Nairobi (later renamed the Kenya National Museum). The position paid very little, but Louis and Mary were able to live in the official curator's house.

During the war, the archaeological work was even more challenging. Gasoline rationing prevented the Leakeys from doing much traveling. Mary was able to work on a site at Naivasha, near Nairobi, but her activities were limited by the birth of their first child, Jonathan Harry Erskine Leakey, born on November 4, 1940. After Jonathan was a bit older, Mary continued her work at several sites. One in particular, a site called Olorgesailie, had fossils and tools that were later dated as 400,000 years old. To help work the site, the Leakeys used Italian prisoners of war, some of whom later settled in the area permanently.

The Leakey family continued to grow. In 1943, Mary had a daughter; the infant died when she was only a few weeks old. The following year, on December 24, Richard Erskine Frere Leakey was born. The Leakeys' last child, Philip, was born after the war, on June 21, 1949.

35

Chapter 4

The Glory Years

Rusinga Island lies just off the northwest coast of Lake Victoria. Louis Leakey first saw Rusinga during a boat trip in 1926 and thought it would be a good site for finding fossils. In 1932, while working at nearby Kanam and Kanjera, he borrowed a boat and explored the island on weekends. He found enough fossils to convince him to return.

Over the next several years, Louis returned to Rusinga for several short visits. In 1942, he found a large piece of jawbone of an extinct ape, later identified as *Proconsul nyanzae*. This was the most complete Miocene ape jaw yet found. Because of World War II, he was not able to publicize this discovery immediately, but it caused quite a stir in 1946.

Louis and Mary and their family spent a good part of 1947 and 1948 on Rusinga. On the morning of October 6, 1948, Mary and Louis explored a gully near where their workers were digging. Mary spotted some bone fragments and a tooth buried in the side of a cliff. She called to Louis, and together they worked for two days to uncover the bones.

Proconsul: A Missing Link?

They had found the skull of a fossil ape, belonging to a species called *Proconsul africanus*. The original owner of the skull had lived almost 20 million years ago, in the early Miocene era. Bits and pieces of this species had been found before, but never a skull like this one.

Once the skull was removed and preserved, Mary boarded an airplane for England. She and her fossil got VIP treatment all the way, including police escorts to and from the airports.

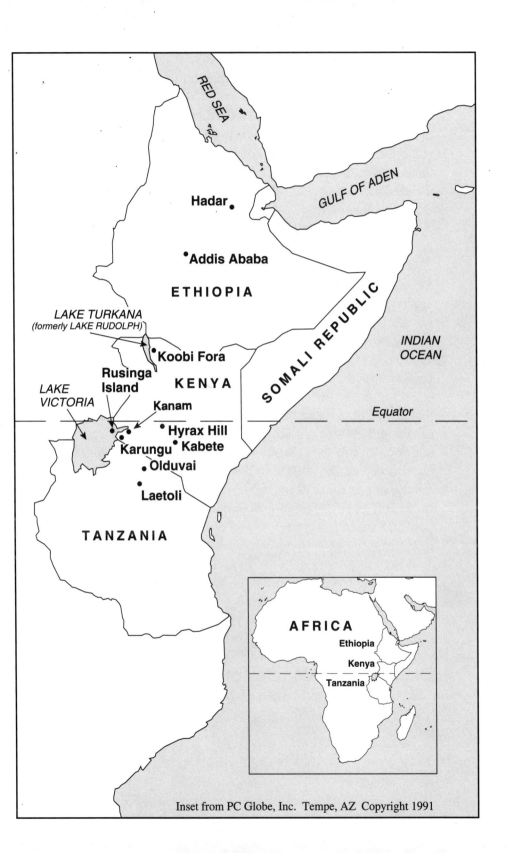

RED SEA

GULF OF ADEN

Hadar •

•Addis Ababa

ETHIOPIA

LAKE TURKANA
(formerly LAKE RUDOLPH)

•Koobi Fora

SOMALI REPUBLIC

INDIAN
OCEAN

Rusinga
Island

KENYA

Kanam

LAKE
VICTORIA

Equator

• Hyrax Hill

Karungu • • Kabete

• Olduvai

Laetoli

TANZANIA

AFRICA

Ethiopia

Kenya

Tanzania

Inset from PC Globe, Inc. Tempe, AZ Copyright 1991

Upon arriving in London, she took the skull to the laboratory of Wilfred Le Gros Clark, a world-famous specialist in the anatomy of prehistoric animals. In his report, he emphasized the combination of both hominid and monkey-like features in the skull. *Proconsul* had a relatively large, ape-like head but lacked the heavy ridges above the eyes that were typical of apes. It had small molar teeth and large canine teeth, and it probably had eaten soft fruits.

The newspapers hailed the discovery as "the missing link," a probable ancestor to both modern humans and apes. Later evidence would suggest that the last ancestor common to both groups lived much more recently, 18 million years ago or perhaps even 5 million years ago. Nevertheless, the discovery was sensational. It also ensured continued funding for future Leakey expeditions.

At the same time, the success of the Leakeys aroused some jealousy. This was aggravated, in part, by Louis Leakey's lack of tact and his strong faith in his own abilities. Yale anthropologist Elwyn Simons once defined the "Louis Leakey Syndrome" as this attitude: "The fossils I [Louis Leakey] find are the important ones and are on the direct line to man, preferably bearing names I have coined, whereas the fossils you find are of lesser importance and are all on side branches of the tree."

After the discovery of the famous *Proconsul* skull, Louis Leaky wrote, "For some time we had both had a hunch—if that is the word for it—that something very important was near at hand." The "hunches" of both Mary and Louis were usually right and led to more exciting discoveries.

Olduvai Gorge: Valley of Treasures

Louis Leakey first visited Olduvai Gorge in 1931, during his third expedition. The purpose of the trip had been to gather information about a skeleton that had been discovered there in

1913 by a German geologist, Dr. Hans Reck. Reck accompanied Louis on his 1931 expedition. Unfortunately, the age they determined for the skeleton, 1 million years, was later shown to be mistaken. The actual age was only 20,000 years. This episode damaged Leakey's reputation but did not shake his enthusiasm for the site itself.

"Olduvai" is the name given to the gorge by the Masai people. It means "place of the wild sisal," and the gorge is covered with sisal, a type of plant used to make ropes. The first European to see the site was an entomologist named Kattwinkel in 1911. He was chasing a butterfly with his net when he fell 300 feet into the gorge. After he dusted himself off, he spotted several fossilized bones, which he took back with him to Germany. These bones inspired Dr. Reck to visit Olduvai.

Louis returned to Olduvai in 1937 with Mary. On his first trip, he had spotted many other fossils and stone tools, and he was anxious to spend more time on the site. They eventually established a permanent base camp and worked on the site for many years.

Although for many years there were no discoveries as spectacular as *Proconsul*, the Leakeys' fame began to grow. Louis, in particular, was in demand as a writer and lecturer. In 1952, he was even approached by Hollywood. Stewart Granger and Deborah Kerr were starring in a film version of H. Rider Haggard's novel *King Solomon's Mines*, set in East Africa in the 1890's. Louis was paid one thousand dollars to serve as the film's technical adviser. He sent the director of the film some Masai weapons and shields. He also sent a very long list of "dos and don'ts," which included exact instructions for trimming the actors' fingernails, as well as the proper method for wiping away perspiration. Louis was supposed to travel to the set, but the trip was canceled after he and the director argued over the use of a mechanical tarantula in the film. The

Louis Leakey with the skull of Zinjanthropus boisei, *"Nutcracker Man," the skull Mary found in July, 1959.* (AP/Wide World Photos)

film company had paid quite a lot of money for the tarantula, but Louis insisted that it not be used, since tarantulas are not naturally found in East Africa.

The Discovery of *Zinjanthropus*

One morning, on July 17, 1959, Mary Leakey went for a walk in Olduvai Gorge with her two Dalmatians, Sally and Victoria. A film crew was due to arrive in a few days to film an excavation right from the start. Louis was in bed with the flu, and Mary had some time on her hands. Mary's walk took her to a site called "FLK," named in the early 1930's after Louis' first wife.

A piece of bone sticking up from the ground caught Mary's eye. She carefully brushed away some of the soil and then spotted two large teeth. She could tell right away that the teeth were hominid. Mary rushed back to camp. Despite his illness, Louis jumped from his bed and joined her at the site. His first reaction was disappointment; he had hoped that the bones and teeth were from a species of *Homo*, but closer inspection revealed a skull more like *Australopithecus.*

The complete excavation of the skull was filmed and later appeared on the British television series *On Safari*. It took Mary eighteen months to piece together all the fragments of the skull. Only a month after the discovery, Louis sent a report to the British journal *Nature*. In his report, Louis wrote, "I am not in favor of creating too many new generic names among the Hominidae, but I believe it is desirable to place the new find in a separate and distinct genus. I therefore propose to name the new skull *Zinjanthropus boisei*." The genus name, *Zinjanthropus*, means "man of East Africa," and the species name was derived from Charles Boise, the man who helped to finance the early Olduvai expeditions. Louis' statement that he did not favor creating too many new names is ironic, because eventually he became known as one of the ultimate "splitters."

41

A splitter is a scientist who believes in creating new genus and species names based on the smallest differences. The opposite of a splitter is a "lumper"—someone who favors combining widely different creatures into relatively few "taxa" (groups).

Among themselves, the Leakeys called the skull "Dear Boy," "Zinj," or "Nutcracker Man" because of his large teeth. Based on potassium-argon dating techniques, the age of the skull was estimated as 1.75 million years old. The discovery of *Zinjanthropus* caused an even greater sensation than the *Proconsul* skull had aroused. Once again, Mary boarded a plane, the carefully wrapped reconstructed skull sitting on her lap. This time the skull was examined by a physical anthropologist, Philip Tobias of the University of Witwatersrand in South Africa. Tobias insisted that the skull did not represent a new genus but was instead a new species of the genus *Australopithecus*. So *Z. boisei* became *A. boisei*.

For the Leakey family, the discovery of Zinj had an even more important impact. In 1960, the National Geographic Society began supporting the Leakeys' work on a large scale. The first of many articles, "Finding the World's Earliest Man," appeared in the September, 1960, issue of *National Geographic Magazine*. These articles and ensuing television specials gained widespread popular support for the Leakeys in the United States. In 1962, both Louis and Mary traveled to the United States to receive the gold Hubbard Award, the National Geographic Society's highest honor.

Homo habilis: The Handy Man

One day in the late autumn of 1960, the Leakeys' oldest son, Jonathan, wandered off from the Zinj site. About 250 yards away he spotted some teeth and a jaw bone, and the whole family became very excited when these proved to come from an extinct saber-toothed tiger, a species never before found at Olduvai. Some of the crew started work on this new

Louis Leakey poses with the jaw and skull fragments from "Jonny's Child." (AP/Wide World Photos)

site, called "Jonny's site." Instead of finding more tiger bones, they found a hominid tooth. Then, on November 2, Jonathan found a lower jaw and two pieces of hominid skull. From the teeth, it was obvious that this individual was young, probably around twelve years old, when he died. His remains were dubbed "Jonny's Child." At the same site, Mary found some hand bones, as well as some other bones belonging to two adults.

The geology at Jonny's site suggested that these newest fossils were even older than Zinj. The bones suggested an individual with a lighter build and a larger brain than Zinj. Adult foot and leg bones proved that these creatures had walked erect. The adults probably stood only three or four feet tall—a revelation that gave rise to misleading headlines in the popular press, such as Pygmy Progenitor. Most important, this creature, rather than Zinj, was probably the maker of many of the stone tools that the Leakeys had found around Olduvai.

In the April 4, 1964, issue of *Nature*, Louis, along with Philip Tobias and anatomist John Napier, published an article titled "A New Species of the Genus *Homo* from Olduvai Gorge." After several years of study, Leakey decided that these most recent fossils were human enough to be called *Homo* but primitive enough to rate a new species name, *habilis*. Habilis means "handy" or "able" and was suggested to Leakey by Professor Raymond Dart, who had discovered the first skull of *Australopithecus africanus*. The ability of *H. habilis* to make tools was a strong argument in favor of the *Homo* classification.

Not everyone was happy with Louis' conclusions. One old friend, Wilfred Le Gros Clark, declared that the fossils could only be australopithecine. Even Tobias and Napier backed away from their conclusions under pressure from other scientists. Louis, however, was convinced that more fossils would be found to support his ideas. In 1971, support for

THE LEAKEYS

Homo habilis would come from Louis and Mary's son,
Richard. His discoveries of *H. habilis* fossils at Koobi Fora,
Kenya, came shortly before Louis Leakey's death.

45

Chapter 5

Footprints in the Past

The discovery of hominid footprints at Laetoli, Tanzania, was one of the most exciting scientific events to occur in the twentieth century. With these footprints in mind, Mary Leakey wrote:

> I cannot help but think about the distant creatures who made them. Where did they come from? Where were they going? We simply do not know. . . . In any case, those footprints out of the deep past, left by the oldest hominids, haunt the imagination. Across the gulf of time I can only wish them well on that prehistoric trek.

The Partnership Ends

Louis Leakey died of a heart attack on October 1, 1972. The last years of his life were painful ones. He suffered from the lingering effects of malaria, a broken hip, and other consequences of a lifetime in the wild. In 1971, he was attacked and stung by several hundred bees, a freak accident that left him partially paralyzed. An operation to remove a clot from his brain relieved the paralysis, but he still had difficulty writing. His poor health made him cranky and fretful.

Mary and Louis were seldom together from 1968 until Louis' death. Mary lived and worked at Olduvai Gorge, and Louis traveled constantly, giving lectures and raising funds. Their separation was prolonged by a disagreement over a professional matter. Louis was involved with a group excavating an 80,000-year-old site at the Calico Hills in the Mojave Desert in southern California. They hoped to find evidence of early humans in America. Louis publicly asserted that flakes of rock found there were certainly human-made artifacts. Mary believed that they were more likely caused by natural processes. To support his claims, Louis assembled an international conference at Calico in October, 1970. None of the experts supported his claim. However, out of respect, affection, and fear for his health (Louis was just recovering from a serious heart attack), no one challenged Louis directly. Although Louis announced that his findings had been "confirmed," he afterward avoided the topic of Calico, as did most obituaries at the time of his death.

Laetoli: Mary Takes a New Path

A few years after Louis died, Mary began work at Laetoli. Laetoli is about thirty miles south of Olduvai, and it is also part of Tanzania. Like "Olduvai," the word "Laetoli" is a Masai word, the name for a type of red lily found there. Mary and Louis had first visited Laetoli in 1935. They were working at Olduvai and running a clinic where they treated the local people for minor illnesses and wounds. One patient told them of a site with "bones like stone" and offered to take them there. They visited the site, gathered some fossils, and recorded the location.

Mary visited Laetoli again briefly several times, but it was not until 1974 that she decided to try any serious work there. With the help of Kamoya Kimeu (leader of Richard Leakey's Kenyan fossil hunters) and other members of Richard Leakey's "Hominid Gang," she explored the site for several weeks and found a number of hominid fossils. Based on these findings, she applied for a grant from the National Geographic Society. The Society was enthusiastic and generous, and Mary and her team began work at Laetoli in July of 1975.

The first few seasons yielded mostly hominid jaws and teeth. Using potassium-argon dating techniques, she and her team found that the age of the fossils was between 3.6 and 3.8 million years old—the oldest hominid fossils yet discovered.

47

Mary needed someone to describe the anatomy of the fossils for publication. She asked Tim White, a doctoral student who had worked with Richard Leakey and who later became a close colleague of another famous paleoanthropologist, Donald Johanson.

Tim White's description stressed the similarity between the Laetoli fossils and younger *Homo habilis* specimens found at other sites. It also pointed out several features that seemed "primitive" or "ape-like." Assigning an appropriate genus and species name to these fossils became even more critical with the discovery of the Laetoli footprints.

Mary (right), with assistant Louise Robbins, displays plaster casts of the Laetoli footprints. (AP/Wide World Photos)

1. Louis Seymour Bazett Leakey. (Marvin E. Newman, Woodfin Camp)

2. Olduvai Gorge, Tanzania. (Wendy Stone, Odyssey)

3. Memorial to the discovery of *Zinjanthropus*, Olduvai Gorge. (Lawrence S. Burr)

4. Louis and Richard at Omo Valley, Ethiopia. (Bob Campbell)

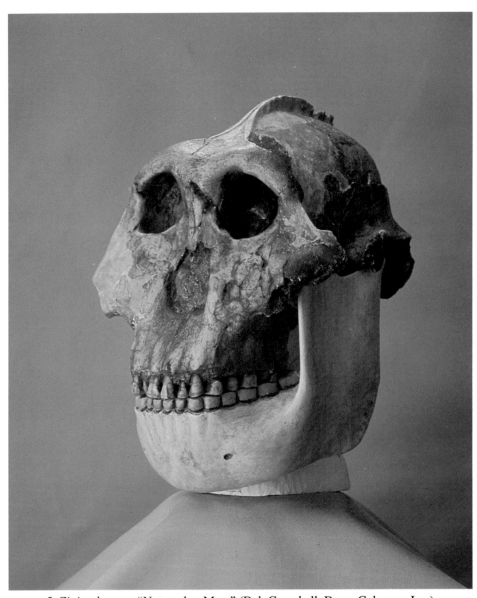

5. *Zinjanthropus*, "Nutcracker Man." (Bob Campbell, Bruce Coleman, Inc.)

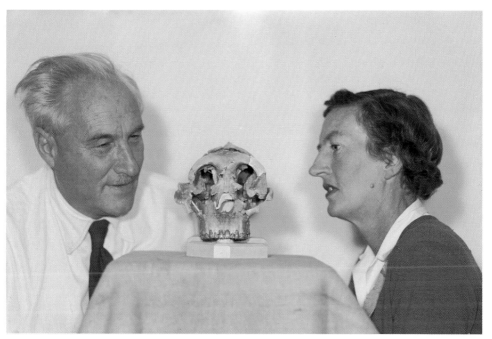

6. Louis and Mary examine *Zinjanthropus*. (Jen and Des Bartlett, Bruce Coleman, Inc.)

7. The countryside of Tanzania. (David Shores, Unicorn Stock Photos)

8. Richard (right) and Kamoya Kimeu, head of the "Hominid Gang," with a *Homo erectus* skull. (Bob Campbell)

9. Richard near Koobi Fora. (Bob Campbell)

10. Richard at the Lake Turkana site. (Delta Willis, Bruce Coleman, Inc.)

11. Richard and Mary compare skulls. (Bob Campbell)

12. Richard working with Meave at Lake Turkana. (Bob Campbell)

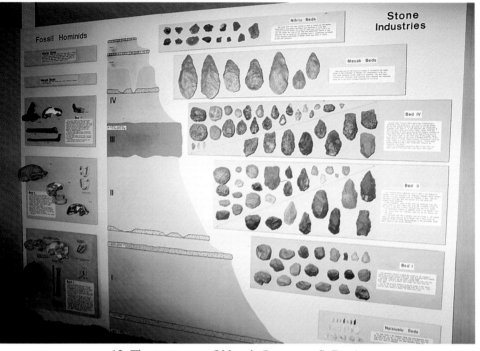

13. The museum at Olduvai. (Lawrence S. Burr)

14. Richard in Nairobi State Park at an ivory-burning ceremony, protesting the slaughter of elephants for their tusks. (Wendy Stone, Odyssey)

The Laetoli Footprints

In 1976, visitors to Laetoli stumbled across some fossilized animal footprints. The footprints included those of insects, birds, and larger animals such as rhinoceroses and elephants. Later, Peter Jones, Mary's assistant, and Philip, Mary's youngest son, found more footprints, including four rather unclear footprints that Mary thought might be those of hominids.

The most exciting discovery came in 1978. Two parallel trails of clear hominid prints were found, again by accident. A visitor, Paul Abell, who also worked closely with Richard, wanted to cut out a block of rhinoceros prints for the Olduvai museum. He found what appeared to be a hominid heel print. Mary agreed that the print was most likely that of a hominid and assigned Ndibo Mbuika, one of her Kenyan workers, to excavate the site. He found two more prints. Then, Tim White took charge of the excavation and found a trail of prints 30 feet long. The next season, more footprints were found, until the trail extended beyond 80 feet.

The rock containing the footprints was dated at 3.6 million years. The footprints are actually those of three individuals, with the middle-sized individual deliberately stepping into the footprints of the largest individual. The most remarkable conclusion from these footprints is the proof of early bipedalism; that is, these small, primitive creatures were walking upright, on two feet, long before *Homo sapiens* or even *Homo erectus*. No tools were ever found at the site, suggesting that bipedalism came before the use of tools.

The classification problem still remained. Mary Leakey saw the fossils and footprints as belonging to human ancestors, possibly *Homo*, not members of the *Australopithecus* line that eventually died out. In an article for *National Geographic*, she wrote,

. . . we have found hominid prints that are remarkably similar to those of modern man. Prints that, in my opinion, could only have been left by an ancestor of man.

Mary Leakey's assessment of the Laetoli fossils was challenged by another paleoanthropologist, Donald Johanson. Johanson was working in Ethiopia, in an area called Hadar in the Afar Triangle. In 1974, Johanson found a hominid skeleton, which the world came to know as Lucy. A year later, he found fragments of at least thirteen additional individuals. Johanson worked closely with the Leakeys for several years, but then he published a paper in 1978 in which he suggested that fossils found at Hadar and Laetoli represented one species, which he named *Australopithecus afarensis*. Mary Leakey had been listed as a co-author, because the paper included descriptions of some Laetoli fossils. She insisted, however, that her name be removed for several reasons. Mary and her son, Richard, felt that the Hadar fossils included at least two different species, one of which might possibly be *Homo* rather than *Australopithecus*. Mary also believed that the creation of a new species name was too sudden and needed further study. The use of Mary's Laetoli fossils as a prototype for a species she did not believe in was, she felt, an insult. Finally, the first she heard of the proposed new name was not from Johanson directly but instead at the Nobel symposium they were both attending.

After Laetoli

Mary Leakey spent only five seasons at Laetoli. In 1980, she returned to Olduvai, visiting Laetoli only occasionally. More and more of her time was spent lecturing, traveling, and fund-raising. In 1977, she began a yearly lecture tour of the United States, sponsored by the Leakey Foundation. Mary was not accustomed to traveling, and she found public speaking a nerve-racking experience. However, like Louis, she found American audiences to be warm and enthusiastic. She especially enjoyed American food, but she never did acquire a taste for hamburgers or for salad, which she called "rabbit food."

In May, 1978, Mary was invited by the Royal Swedish Academy of Sciences to attend a symposium entitled "The Current Argument on Early Man," organized by the Nobel Foundation. At the symposium, she also received the Linnaeus Medal, named for the Swedish scientist Karl Linnaeus, who first established the system for creating genus and species names.

It was at this symposium that the dramatic break between the Leakeys and Donald Johanson and Tim White occurred. Mary Leakey's relationship with Johanson and White had been cordial up to that point. The break actually started when he (Johanson) spoke at length about the Laetoli fossils in a speech just before Mary's own talk about the fossils. In his speech, he gave details, for the first time, of the proposed new species name that was to be published in the article to which Mary's name had been added. It was after the symposium that she insisted that her name be removed from the paper, and it was at that point that the feud began.

Mary received several honorary degrees from distinguished universities, including Yale and the University of Chicago. In 1981, she was awarded an honorary degree of doctor of letters by Oxford University in England, an honor Louis had received in 1950. She found the degrees ironic, since she had not been able to enroll in a university in her youth. She also found the pomp and ceremonies amusing; she was never a woman who valued formality or convention.

In 1982, while in camp at Olduvai, Mary woke up one morning with vision in only her right eye. When this persisted the next day, her son Jonathan arranged for her to see a

Mary and Dr. Melvin Payne, chair of the National Geographic Society's Committee for Research and Exploration, examine the Laetoli footprints. (AP/Wide World Photos)

specialist in Nairobi. The problem turned out to be a blood clot that had lodged behind her left eye. Had it settled in her brain or heart, it could have caused her death. As it was, she permanently lost the sight in her left eye.

Not long after her eye trouble developed, Mary decided to move from Olduvai to Nairobi. In the mid-1980's she assigned the care of Olduvai to the Tanzanian Department of Antiquities. She then undertook several writing projects, including publication of her autobiography, *Disclosing the Past* (1984).

Chapter 6

The Second Generation

One trait the Leakeys seem to share is loyalty. This loyalty extends even to the family pets, of which there have always been many. On one expedition, Richard Leakey's favorite dog, Ben, wandered away. A quick search failed to find him, and Richard decided that only an aerial search could help. He drove to a nearby town and tried to charter a plane. When told that all aircraft were booked, Richard explained that a member of his expedition was lost. The company canceled a reservation to make a plane available at once, and Ben was found later that day.

The Leakey Children

After Louis and Frida Leakey were divorced, their children, Priscilla and Colin, did not see their father until they were adults. Eventually, both children and their families formed ties with Louis and his new family. Priscilla trained as a physiotherapist and married a schoolteacher, Justin Davies. They and their children, Alison and Andrew, visited Kenya at Christmas in 1962.

Colin attended King's College, Cambridge, and specialized in botany. Eventually, he earned his doctorate. In 1961, he married physical education teacher Susan Marshall, and they later had three daughters, Emma, Tess, and Tamsin. That same year, Colin accepted a teaching post at Makerere University in what is now Uganda. He and his family lived in Uganda until September, 1972, when they left because of political unrest. Colin was in London when Louis Leakey died on October 1, and he released word of his father's death to the media.

Louis and Mary Leakey had three sons, Jonathan, Richard, and Philip. Louis was actively involved in their upbringing. When Jonathan was a baby, Louis happily changed diapers and prepared bottles while Mary was away fossil-hunting.

Louis displays the fossil remains of Homo habilis *("Jonny's Child"); other anthropologists did not at first accept Leakey's judgment that he had discovered a new ancestor of human beings.* (AP/Wide World Photos)

Jonathan seemed to take after Mary and was a quiet, studious boy. While young, he developed an interest in snakes. After secondary school, Jonathan established a snake park in Nairobi, near the museum where Louis was curator. He also was a frequent visitor at his parents' excavation sites. It was on such a visit that he found the first *Homo habilis* fossils. In 1963, he married Mollie Knights-Rayson, and they settled in Kenya, raising snakes and melons. Jonathan and Mollie's first child, Julia, was Mary Leakey's first grandchild.

Philip Leakey is the youngest of the Leakey children. Unlike his brother Jonathan, Philip did not care much for school. When he was sixteen, Philip was sent to school in England. He was very homesick and returned to Kenya after only one term. Philip tried a number of different ventures. For a while, he ran a safari company, like his brother Richard. Inspired by his half-brother Colin, Philip collected orchids. In 1964, he accompanied his brother Richard on one of his first fossil-hunting expeditions. Like his brothers, he often visited his parents as they worked. Philip and his wife Valerie settled in Nairobi, where Philip became the only white official in the Kenyan government. In 1979, shortly after his first election to the Kenyan Parliament, Philip donated one of his kidneys to his older brother, Richard.

The Heir to the Kingdom

Of all the Leakey children, Richard Erskine Frere Leakey has been the only one to pursue a career in paleoanthropology. Like his father, Richard was born in Kenya, while it was still a British colony. His early years were spent playing with his brothers, fishing, swimming, and hunting for birds' nests.

Richard started school when he was five years old. At first, he attended Catholic schools, and then he went to Nairobi Primary School. For high school, he was a day student at the same boarding school as his brothers, but he was not very happy. He preferred exploring and horseback riding to studying. He also had problems with some of the other students at the school, whose families were angered by Louis Leakey's support for populist leader and future prime minister

Jomo Kenyatta and his nationalist movement.

Richard discovered his first fossil when he was only six years old. His parents were working at Kanjera, on the shore of Lake Victoria. One morning, when Richard was pestering his parents as they worked, Louis told Richard to go dig up his own bone. Richard got some dental picks and a small brush and promptly found a bone. His parents worried when he was

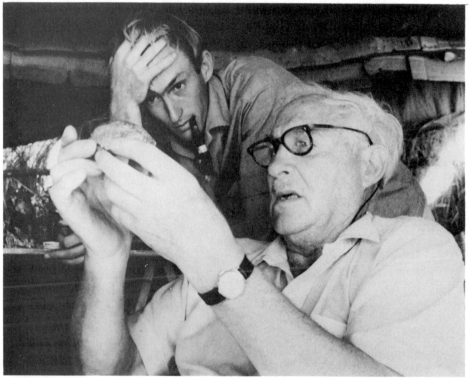

Louis and son Richard puzzle over the identity of a bone fragment. (AP/Wide World Photos)

quiet for so long and were surprised to find him happily working on excavating the jawbone of a giant pig. It was the most complete specimen of that species yet found, and young Richard was quickly shoved aside. This made him very angry.

In his autobiography, *One Life*, Richard suggests that this incident may have alienated him from the formal study of anthropology

When Richard was thirteen, he began earning money by trapping wild animals. He started with small animals such as mongooses, porcupines, and bush babies (small, tree-climbing primates) for nature films. When he was sixteen, he helped local game wardens trap a pride of lions that had moved into a Nairobi suburb.

Richard also tried to trap a leopard but instead got trapped himself. He set a trap consisting of a large cage with a live goat as bait. One night he checked his trap and spotted the leopard only twenty feet away and ready to pounce. Richard quickly jumped in the cage and slammed the door. He and the goat spent the night in the trap, until they were released the next day by a search party.

Safaris and Expeditions

Shortly after he was graduated from school, Richard started a company to run safaris, with himself acting as a guide. One of his first clients was the National Geographic Society, which hired him to establish a camp at Olduvai for a television team. Over the next several years, Richard continued to visit his parents frequently while traveling all over East Africa. He learned to fly a plane, earning his pilot's license in 1963. Flying over Lake Natron in Tanzania, he spotted some cliffs along the shore that looked like the rock formations at Olduvai. A short visit proved that these rocks also held fossils. As a result, and supported by Louis and Mary's National Geographic funds, Richard led his first archaeological expedition in early 1964.

Besides Richard, the expedition included nine other people. Philip Leakey accompanied his brother, as well as a professional archaeologist, Glynn Isaac, who worked at the

Coryndon Museum with Louis Leakey. The photographer was Hugo van Lawick, who later worked with Jane Goodall and her chimpanzees. The remaining members were Kenyans, one of whom, Kamoya Kimeu, became a close friend and colleague of Richard. Kamoya made the first important discovery, a complete lower jaw of a hominid of the species *Australopithecus boisei*. After the jaw was collected, the expedition returned to Olduvai long enough to raise funds for a lengthier trip. The National Geographic Society agreed to support a three-month dig, planned for that summer.

Richard organized the trip and Glynn Isaac was the chief scientist. A few students also came along, including Margaret Cropper of the University of Edinburgh in Scotland. Margaret had worked for a while at Olduvai and had briefly dated Jonathan Leakey. She and Richard became quite close during the expedition, and they were married two years later.

Richard enjoyed the expedition; he found it more satisfying than catering to the whims of tourists. However, he realized that without a college degree, it would be difficult to contribute to the scientific side of the work. So, in 1965, he enrolled in a program in London to help him prepare for college entrance examinations. After six months of studying physics, chemistry, and biology, he passed the exams. It was too late to enroll for that fall, and his safari business needed attention, so he returned to Kenya.

In 1966, Richard organized an expedition to Baringo, Kenya. Jonathan Leakey owned a nearby farm and had alerted Louis Leakey to the presence of fossils in the area. Louis organized a short scouting trip which confirmed the potential of the site. Richard persuaded Louis to let him lead the first full-scale expedition. Richard was helped by his new wife, Margaret, who had just obtained her degree in archaeology.

The expedition proved to be so interesting that Richard forgot to apply for admission to college and the deadline

Relative Dating Techniques

In order to understand which fossil came before which, a reliable way of dating the fossils is needed. Fossils are usually found in groups: When a hominid fossil is found in a layer of rock, there are usually many fossils of other animals found in the same layer of rock. Pigs, for example, are found nearly everywhere, and their evolutionary history is very well known. Paleontologist Basil Cooke is a specialist in prehistoric "suids": members of the pig family. His studies have helped develop a "yardstick" based on pig development. A paleontologist can tell the relative age of a new hominid fossil by comparing it to the type of pig fossils found with it.

This method is a type of relative dating. It does not give us the fossil's absolute age; it can only tell us that this fossil is older or younger than another one. Other relative dating methods rely on geological events, such as volcanic eruptions or the reversing of the earth's magnetic field.

Absolute Dating Techniques

Many absolute dating techniques rely on the "decay rates" of radioactive isotopes. Scientists can tell how old certain atoms are by how fast they change from one type of element to another. In one method, the decay of an atom of carbon 14 can be used to date some bones, but only those 50,000 years old or younger. For older specimens, radioactive argon decay rates are used. Argon can be found trapped in pieces of volcanic rock. Argon is a gas, so the rock is first heated in an oven to release the argon gas. The argon gas is absorbed by charcoal, and then it is rapidly chilled. The argon is then ionized in a machine called a mass spectrophotometer. Magnets in the machine direct argon ions onto a target. The number of "hits" on the target can be used to calculate the age of the sample.

Still another method is called thermoluminescence. Many rocks are able to absorb radiation from the atmosphere. When these rocks are heated, this energy is released as light energy, and the rock's "clock" is set to zero. Using a device called a photomultiplier, scientists can heat even a few small grains of a sample and measure the light given off. Using this method, they can tell how much time has passed since the sample was last heated—perhaps when a stone spearhead was kicked into a prehistoric campfire.

passed. Although the subject came up again several different times, Richard never had the desire to spend the years away from Africa that a degree would require. While the lack of a formal degree caused him some difficulties, he never regretted his decision.

Chapter 7

The Bones of Lake Turkana

Lake Turkana, once known as Lake Rudolf, is located in a remote part of Kenya, more than fifty miles from the nearest village. The area is now part of a thousand-square-mile national park that includes most of the eastern shore of the lake. In order to transport people and equipment to expedition sites, Richard Leakey has employed nearly every type of vehicle. Trucks, boats, helicopters, and planes have all been used. Even camels have occasionally been pressed into service as a convenient, though temperamental, means of travel.

The Omo Valley

The Omo River crosses the southern part of Ethiopia and joins with Lake Turkana. In the early part of the twentieth century, several French expeditions had gathered thousands of pounds of fossils from the valley around the river. After World War II, foreign expeditions were prohibited until 1966.

With the help of Jomo Kenyatta, the first president of the newly independent Kenya, Louis Leakey persuaded Ethiopia's Emperor Haile Selassie to allow an international expedition to look for fossils in the Omo Valley. The countries represented were Ethiopia, Kenya, France, and the United States. Louis chose Richard to be the field leader of the Kenyan team and to act as Louis' representative. Other members of the Kenyan team included Richard's wife Margaret, Paul Abell, and Kamoya Kimeu. The National Geographic Society agreed to support the project, and the expedition was planned for the summer of 1967.

The expedition was successful in finding fossils, but for

Richard Leakey it was a frustrating experience. The French team found an australopithecine jaw, older than similar jaws found previously at Olduvai. The American team found a fossil bed from the Pliocene age, dated between 2 million and 3.5 million years old. The Kenyans were disappointed because their assigned area contained beds no more than 150,000 years old. Kamoya Kimeu did find a *Homo sapiens* skull about 130,000 years old. This find proved to be an important one, because it suggested that Neanderthals, a sub-type of *Homo sapiens*, were cousins, not ancestors, of modern humans.

While Richard was working on the Omo expedition, he flew back to Nairobi for a week to attend to his safari business. Because of a thunderstorm, the pilot made a detour and flew low over the eastern shore of Lake Turkana. From his window, Richard spotted some areas that seemed to "shout" fossils. On returning to Omo, he borrowed a helicopter from the Americans for a day and explored the region more thoroughly. Everywhere he went he saw fossils. Richard decided that this was the area that he would make his own—no more working with or under other people, especially his parents.

At the end of the season, Richard traveled to Washington, D.C., to report to the National Geographic Society's Committee for Research and Exploration. Much to everyone's surprise, he did not ask for money to plan a second expedition to the Omo Valley. Instead, he asked for, and received, $25,000 to explore the eastern shore of Lake Turkana in Kenya.

Lake Turkana: Shores of Fossils

In the summer of 1968, the first expedition left Nairobi for Lake Turkana. The Kenyan Minister of State, a Kikuyu and a friend of Louis Leakey, sent along an armed escort to protect the group from bands of raiders present along the Kenya-Ethiopia border.

Starting June 10, Richard and his handpicked group of

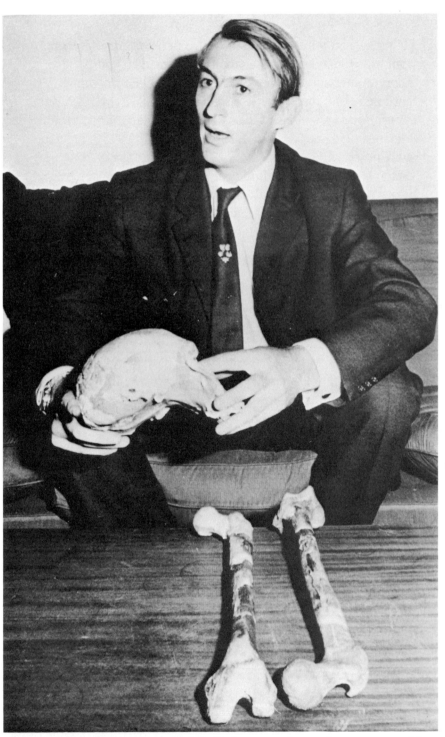

Richard Leakey with bones from the Lake Turkana area that are between two and three million years old. (AP/Wide World Photos)

scientists and assistants began to explore the Lake Turkana
area. A typical day began at sunrise. Everyone worked until
noon, when it became too hot to walk about. The team rested
until three and then began exploring again. They saw
thousands of fossils, mostly dating from the Pliocene or
Pleistocene ages. Three hominid specimens were found, as
well as numerous examples of other species. The only
disappointment was their inability to find the site Richard had
visited by helicopter; in his excitement, he had failed to note
the location properly. Otherwise, the expedition was a
complete success.

In early 1969, Richard returned to Washington, D.C., to
report to the National Geographic Society on the Lake Turkana
expedition. While visiting, he raised funds for a second
expedition and recruited a young geologist, Kay
Behrensmeyer, to work on the site. Shortly after he returned to
Kenya, Richard and Margaret's daughter Anna was born.

The Kenya National Museum

In 1968, Richard was appointed Administrative Director of
the Kenya National Museum, formerly the Coryndon Museum.
This appointment was part of a long campaign to put more
native Kenyans in control of the nation's treasures and
resources. Louis Leakey had resigned as curator in 1961, when
he established a separate Centre for Prehistory and
Paleontology. After a long battle with the museum's board of
directors, Richard finally gained the post he wanted. He was
then able to make changes, to increase the number of Kenyan
employees, and to ensure that all fossils found in Kenya stayed
in Kenya, under the control of the museum. He also insisted
that many of the Olduvai fossils be returned to Tanzania, a
decision that angered Louis greatly.

While Richard's new post at the museum improved both his
financial and his academic positions, other parts of his life

were not proceeding as smoothly. While on his way to the United States in 1969, Richard visited a London specialist and learned that his kidneys were permanently damaged from an infection that he had suffered that fall. The doctor told him that his kidneys would probably fail in about ten years and recommended a special diet and frequent check-ups. Richard decided to keep this information a secret from all but his wife and to live as normal a life as possible for as long as possible. He managed to do so until 1979, when his kidneys finally failed. A kidney transplant saved his life. The kidney came from his brother Philip, who immediately volunteered to be a donor once Richard's problem became known.

Richard also had domestic problems. His decision to ignore his kidney problems upset Margaret. Also, she believed that, at age twenty-five, he was too young and inexperienced for the museum post. Other differences developed, and in late 1969 they separated, then divorced.

Koobi Foora: Early Tool Makers

The second expedition to Lake Turkana started in the summer of 1969. The team members were slightly different; Margaret stayed home with daughter Anna, but the group was joined by geologist Kay Behrensmeyer and zoologist Meave Gillian Epps. They chose to make camp at a sandy peninsula called Koobi Foora.

One of Behrensmeyer's tasks was to look for volcanic material that could be dated using potassium-argon techniques. While she was working, she spotted some lava flakes that proved to be the first stone tools found in that area. The site was promptly named the Kay Behrensmeyer site (KBS, for short), and the volcanic "tuff" (clumped volcanic ash) around the tools was sent to England to be dated. The results came back: The tools were an incredible 2.4 million years old, nearly 500,000 years older than any tools yet found. The dating of the

KBS tuff started a controversy that would last for more than a decade. More refined dating techniques eventually set the age closer to 1.89 million years, but that was still significantly older than any tools previously found.

The discovery of the stone tools encouraged everyone to search for the hominid who had made the tools. Richard found the skull of an *Australopithecus boisei*, but a more spectacular discovery at Koobi Foora was made three years later.

The Discovery of Skull 1470

The year 1972 was an important one for Richard Leakey. In 1971 he had married Meave Epps, and in March, 1972, their first daughter, Louise, was born. A second daughter, Samira, was born in 1974. When Louise was only six weeks old, she accompanied her parents on their yearly trip to Koobi Foora. This trip was highlighted by the discovery of the skull known as KNM-ER 1470 (its record number with the Kenya National Museum).

Over the years, Richard Leakey gathered a group of highly skilled native Kenyans to work as assistants on his expeditions. This group, known as the Hominid Gang, was responsible for many of the most important fossil discoveries of Koobi Foora. Bernard Ngeneo, a member of this special group, first spotted the pieces of a skull in late July, 1972. The skull was in many tiny pieces, which were retrieved by carefully sifting through the sand at the site. It took many weeks to collect all the pieces, and many more for Meave to put all the pieces together. When it was done, Richard showed the skull to his father, the morning before Louis left for England. Louis was delighted; it was a *Homo habilis* skull, an example of the species he had named. Two days later, Louis Leakey died.

83

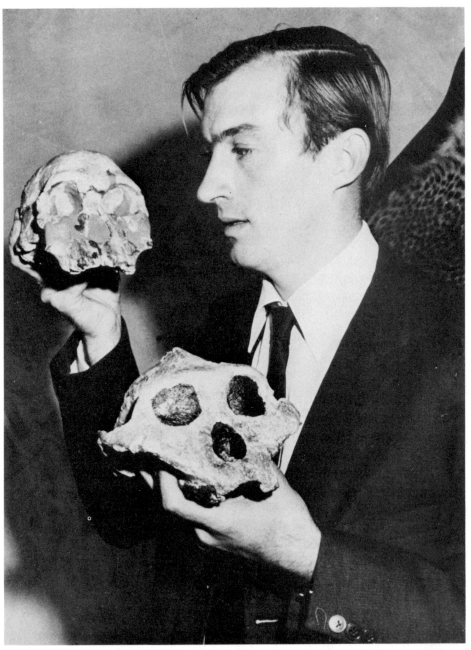

Richard Leakey, in 1972, displays "Skull 1470" (top), two to three million years old, and the skull of a one-million-year-old Australopithecus *(bottom).* (AP/Wide World Photos)

Other Important Discoveries

While the 1470 skull received great publicity, more recent discoveries are of equal importance. In 1975, a skull known as 3733 was also found by Bernard Ngeneo. It took several days to remove the buried skull, which was very heavy because the inside was filled with rock. Once the complete skull was visible, it became obvious that the skull was a specimen of *Homo erectus*, buried in rocks more than 1.5 million years old.

An even more exciting discovery was made in 1984. Kamoya Kimeu was scouting a riverbed west of Lake Turkana when he spotted another *Homo erectus* skull. Over a three-week period, the team worked to reveal the nearly complete skeleton of a twelve-year-old boy, later named Turkana Boy. The skeleton was the oldest yet found, 1.6 million years old, and the oldest complete collection of the bones of one individual. Another surprising feature of the skeleton was its size: At the time of his death, the boy stood about 5 feet, 4 inches tall and weighed about 143 pounds. Had he lived, he might have reached six feet in height. Richard Leakey commented, "We used to think of our ancestors as rather puny, even fragile. Perhaps they were much stronger and better built than we had ever imagined."

The Future of Our Past

In the late 1980's and early 1990's, the Leakeys shifted their focus to a site called Lothagam Hill on the western side of Lake Turkana. This site has fossils dating between 4 and 5.5 million years of age. Discovery of a hominid of this age would help answer two questions: "When did humans and apes diverge?" and "When did our ancestors begin to walk erect?" A number of primate fossils have been found at this site, but the search for hominids continues.

Although the Leakeys have shifted their attention to the western shore of Lake Turkana, Koobi Foora now boasts a field school, run by Harvard University. Every summer, two six-week sessions introduce students to field research in paleoanthropology. The head instructor of archaeology is Dr. Harold V. Merrick. When Richard Leakey led the Kenyans on the international expedition to the Omo Valley in Ethiopia, Merrick led the American team. The school is co-sponsored by the National Museums of Kenya.

While Richard Leakey is best known for his work with fossils, he is also very concerned about living creatures, especially endangered species. As the director of Kenya's Wildlife Service, he has worked hard to save the African elephant. In an interview on American television in 1992, Richard said

> We have to . . . stand up for conservation and make sure that these species are preserved.

Chapter 8

The Leakey Legacy

While Louis Leakey is best known for his work in paleoanthropology, he was always a man of many interests. One such interest was primatology. Just as anthropology is the study of humans, primatology is the study of primates. Primatologists study the closest living relatives of human begins, including the chimpanzees, the gorillas, and the orangutans. Louis Leakey believed that studying other primates would help scientists to learn more about human behavior and about the behavior of our extinct ancestors.

Louis Leakey knew that it would take many years in the wild to conduct a thorough study of the behavior of the primates. He did not have that kind of time; instead, he searched for people who loved animals and who could do without the comforts of civilization. He sponsored many different students, but three special women became spectacularly successful.

Leakey's Foster Daughter: Jane Goodall

Louis first looked for someone to study chimpanzees. He found Jane Morris Goodall. In 1957, when Jane was only twenty-three, she traveled to Kenya and met Louis Leakey. He hired her as his secretary, then persuaded her to tackle the chimpanzee project. Louis arranged for her to study at the primate unit at a hospital in London and to work for a year at a London zoo. In 1960, Jane and her mother traveled to the Gombe Stream Reserve on the eastern shore of Lake Tanganyika in Tanzania.

Jane Goodall's work was exciting. She was able to observe

chimps making and using tools. She was also able to document the relationships between the different members of a troop of chimpanzees. Over the years, she became head of her own institute for the study of chimpanzees, and she wrote many books and articles. One colleague even compared the impact of her work to that of Albert Einstein in physics.

Louis Leakey was very proud of Jane. He considered her a foster daughter and arranged for her funding, her doctorate at Cambridge University, and even her first marriage, to Hugo van Lawick, a noted photographer who filmed Louis at Olduvai for a National Geographic program. In later years, Jane has been especially active in fund-raising and ensuring the proper treatment of both captive and wild chimpanzees.

Friend of the Gorillas: Dian Fossey

Dian Fossey first met Louis Leakey in 1963, when she traveled as a tourist to Olduvai. At first, Louis thought of her as "bothersome"; while visiting, she fell, sprained her ankle, and broke a fossil bone. That same year, she traveled with Alan Root, Richard Leakey's safari partner, when he photographed mountain gorillas. She wrote a newspaper article about her observations, which Louis Leakey later read. In 1965, Louis visited Dian during one of his annual American tours. He volunteered to find money for her if she would agree to study mountain gorillas. Dian promptly quit her job as a physiotherapist at a hospital in Kentucky and began preparations for her work.

Dian Fossey started in Zaire, but unrest in that country caused her to move her research to Albert National Park in Rwanda. Much of her early work was supported by the National Geographic Society. She quickly came to love the mountain gorillas—so much so that she started a crusade against the poachers who hunted them. In 1978, she established the Digit Fund to preserve the gorillas and their

Above, Louis Leakey measures the skull of Zinjanthropus boisei. *At right, an artist's conception of how "Nutcracker Man" might have appeared, prepared under Leakey's direction.* (AP/Wide World Photos)

habitat; the fund was named after a favorite gorilla who had been killed by poachers. To help raise public interest in the gorillas, she also wrote a book, *Gorillas in the Mist* (1983). Later the actress Sigourney Weaver portrayed Dian Fossey in a feature film of the same title.

Dian Fossey was found murdered in her cabin in Rwanda on December 26, 1985, presumably killed by the poachers she had fought so vigorously.

Biruté Galdikas and the Red Apes

Unlike Jane Goodall and Dian Fossey, Biruté Galdikas started her career with a college education. She first met Louis Leakey when she was a graduate student in anthropology at the University of California at Los Angeles. Louis lectured to her class one day, and she told him of her interest in orangutans. Two and a half years later, Louis finally scraped together nine thousand dollars from different sources. Biruté and her first husband, photographer Rod Brindamour, left for Indonesia with only enough supplies to fit into two backpacks.

Biruté established camp in Tanjung Puting Reserve on the south coast of Borneo in November of 1971. In the Malay language, *orangutan* means "person of the forest." Unlike chimpanzees and gorillas, who travel in groups, orangutans are solitary. It took Biruté six months to accustom a single animal to her presence. She kept careful notes, recording the behavior she observed minute by minute. Her 333-page doctoral thesis, dedicated to the memory of Louis Leakey, was praised as a monumental contribution.

Like Jane Goodall and Dian Fossey, Biruté Galdikas is dedicated to the preservation of the species she studies. She has been particularly active in helping captive orangutans return to the wild.

Donald Johanson: Lucy and the First Family

Besides Richard and Meave Leakey, there are many others working in the field to add to our knowledge of human evolution. Donald Johanson is one of the better-known researchers. His best-selling book *Lucy: The Beginnings of Mankind* is a popular account of his work in Ethiopia, at Hadar in the Afar Triangle.

When Johanson was a high school student, the *National Geographic* articles about the Leakeys excited him. On the advice of a friend, he entered the University of Illinois as a chemistry major. Soon, however, he switched to anthropology and spent his summers as a journeyman archaeologist on expeditions in the United States. Johanson continued his education in anthropology, receiving both an M.A. and a Ph.D. from the University of Chicago. At Chicago, he worked with another famous paleoanthropologist, F. Clark Howell.

In 1971, Johanson was nearing the end of his studies. He had spent several seasons in Ethiopia at the Omo site, where work had continued even after Richard Leakey's departure. At a party, Johanson met French geologist Maurice Tieb. Tieb was planning a trip to Hadar in the Afar Triangle. On an earlier trip, he had seen many fossils but had no idea what they were. Tieb invited Johanson to examine the site. With money advanced from Case Western Reserve University, Johanson managed to visit Hadar, even before he finished his dissertation. Just as Richard Leakey knew that Koobi Foora was to be "his" site, Johanson fell in love with Hadar.

Upon returning to the United States, Johanson got his degree, started teaching at Case Western, and planned his return to Hadar. With a grant from the National Science Foundation, Johanson, Tieb, and French paleontologist Yves Coppens launched a joint expedition in the fall of 1973. In the first season, Johanson found a 3-million-year-old hominid knee joint. In the second season, he found Lucy, the skeleton

Mary Leakey uses her hands to frame a photograph of one of the Laetoli footprints. (AP/ Wide World Photos)

named for the character in the Beatles' song "Lucy in the Sky with Diamonds." In his third season, Johanson found the "First Family" at a site in which the bones of at least thirteen individuals were mixed together. Obviously, Johanson has a touch of the Leakey luck, too.

Unfortunately, political problems in Ethiopia prevented expeditions to this prolific site for several years after the discovery of the First Family. Johanson settled in Berkeley, California, where he became the director of the Institute of Human Origins.

Africa: The Cradle of Modern Humans?

In Zaire, another husband-and-wife team is working on a site that may contain the earliest evidence of modern human culture. In 1988, Alison Brooks and John Yellen found bone harpoon points at a site called Katanda, a hillside by the Semliki River near Uganda. These carefully crafted tools looked very much like those found in Europe at sites dating near the end of the Paleolithic period, about 14,000 years ago. Using a sophisticated dating technique called thermoluminescence, archaeologists have discovered that the site in Zaire is probably more than 70,000 years old. Previously, most scientists assumed that the characteristics of modern culture (art, sophisticated tools, and ornamentation) began during the Ice Age in Europe, approximately 40,000 years ago. Louis Leakey always believed that the first human ancestors came from Africa. The evidence from Katanda suggests that the first human culture may have started there as well.

A Molecular Approach

Some scientists are taking a completely different approach to research on human origins. Molecular biologists work in laboratories, not dry riverbeds. They study complex protein

Richard Leakey exhibits the reconstructed skull of "Skull 1470." (AP/Wide World Photos)

molecules, including DNA, the material that determines our inherited traits: whether our hair will be blond or brown, for example, or how many teeth we will have. All proteins are made up of combinations of building blocks called amino acids. The sequence of those amino acids is determined by a code or blueprint contained in the structure of the DNA molecule.

In 1967, two scientists from the University of California at Berkeley shocked the scientific world. Vincent Sarich and Allan Wilson studied proteins from chimpanzees, gorillas, and humans. They found that the protein sequences were very similar. Sarich and Wilson concluded that all three groups shared a common ancestor as recently as 5 million years ago (which is very recent in terms of animal evolution). More evidence from other proteins and from studies comparing DNA sequences supports this date.

Paleoanthropologists initially distrusted the molecular approach because it seemed to contradict the fossil evidence. With new dating techniques, however, the two types of evidence—molecular and fossil—seem to be correlating more closely.

Foundation Activities

The L. S. B. Leakey Foundation for Research Related to Man's Origin was formed March 26, 1968. The initial aim of the foundation was to provide money for Louis Leakey's own projects and others he found interesting. After Louis' death, the foundation continued to fund research, support the education of students, and sponsor conferences and publications. The foundation still concentrates on paleoanthropological studies and behavioral studies of primates. It also publishes a newsletter, *AnthroQuest*, which updates contributors on the progress of the foundation's many projects.

Richard Leakey also started a group to support his research, the Foundation for Research into the Origins of Man (FROM), and has been active in fund-raising and has sponsored many important conferences.

Time Line

1903   Louis Seymour Bazett Leakey is born on August 7, in Kabete, Kenya.

1913   Mary Douglas Nicol is born on February 6, in London, England.

1920   In January, Louis enters Weymouth College, a public school (private high school) in England.

1922   Louis enters St. John's College, Cambridge, and begins a modern language tripos.

1923   Louis goes on his first archaeological field trip, with W. E. Cutler, to Tanganyika.

1926   Louis is graduated from Cambridge and heads his own field trip to Kenya with one assistant.

1927   On July 16, Louis' first scientific paper, "Stone Age Man in Kenya Colony," appears in the journal *Nature*.

1928   Louis marries Henrietta Wilfrida (Frida) Avern.

1931   Louis' first child, Priscilla Muthoni, is born. Louis first visits Olduvai Gorge.

1933   Louis' first son, Colin Louis, is born. Louis and Mary meet for the first time. Louis' first book, *Adam's Ancestors*, is published.

1936   Louis and Frida divorce; Louis and Mary are married on December 24.

1940   Jonathan Harry Erskine Leakey is born on November 4. Louis Leakey becomes curator of the Coryndon Museum in Nairobi, Kenya.

1944   Richard Erskine Frere Leakey is born on December 24.

1948   Mary and Louis find the skull of *Proconsul africanus*.

1949   Philip Leakey is born on June 21.

1950   Louis receives an honorary doctor of letters degree from Oxford University.

1957   Louis hires Jane Morris Goodall as his secretary.

1959   Mary discovers the skull of *Zinjanthropus boisei*, later renamed *Australopithecus boisei*. The event is filmed and later appears on British television.

1960   The National Geographic Society begins its long support of the Leakey family. The first article on the Leakeys' work in *National Geographic*, "Finding the World's Earliest Man," appears in September. The first *Homo habilis* skull is discovered, but its importance is not recognized until later. Jane Goodall leaves for her first trip to Tanzania to study chimpanzees.

1961   Louis resigns as curator of the Coryndon Museum; he starts his own Centre for Prehistory and Paleontology.

1962   Louis and Mary receive the gold Hubbard Award, the National Geographic Society's highest honor.

1963   Dian Fossey meets Louis Leakey while on safari in Africa.

1964   Louis co-authors the article in which the name *Homo habilis* is announced. Richard goes on his first expedition to Lake Natron.

1965   Louis meets Dian Fossey during an American tour.

1966   Richard marries Margaret Cropper.

1967   Richard leads the Kenya team on an international expedition to the Omo Valley in Ethiopia. Dian Fossey begins studying gorillas in Rwanda.

1968   Richard leads his first expedition to Lake Turkana; he is appointed Administrative Director of the Kenya National Museum. The L. S. B. Leakey Foundation for Research Related to Man's Origin is established.

1969   Louis and Biruté Galdikas meet. Richard and Margaret's daughter, Anna, is born. Richard and Margaret separate.

1970   Louis assembles an international conference at Calico Hills, California.

1971   Richard marries Meave Epps. Biruté and her husband, Rod Brindamour, arrive in Borneo to begin Project Orangutan.

1972   Louis dies on October 1, in London, England. Richard and Bernard Ngeneo discover *Homo habilis* skull 1470 at Koobi Foora, in Kenya. Richard and Meave's first daughter, Louise, is born.

1974   Richard and Meave's second daughter, Samira, is born. Paleoanthropoligist David Johanson, working in Ethiopia, discovers a hominid skeleton that comes to be known as Lucy.

1975   Mary begins work at Laetoli.

1978   3.6-million-year-old hominid footprints are found at Laetoli. Mary receives the Linnaeus Medal from the Swedish Royal Academy of Sciences.

1979   Richard has a kidney transplant; brother Philip is the donor. Richard's autobiography, *One Life*, is published.

1981   Mary receives an honorary doctorate of letters degree from Oxford University.

1982   Mary loses part of her vision.

1984   Richard and Kamoya Kimeu discover a nearly complete *Homo erectus* skeleton called Turkana Boy. Mary's autobiography *Disclosing the Past* is published.

Important Discoveries

Discovery	Date	Discoverer	Location	Significance
Proconsul africanus	1948	Mary Leakey	Rusinga Island	This 18-million-year-old skull of a prehominid is one of the most complete ever found, a possible ancestor of humans, great apes, and the lesser apes.
Zinjanthropus (*Australopithecus boisei*)	1959	Mary Leakey	Olduvai Gorge	This 1.75-million-year-old skull was the first of its species ever found. The discovery attracted much attention from the public and prompted the National Geographic Society to offer its support. Scientists agree that *A. boisei* is on an evolutionary side branch and is not a human ancestor.
Jonny's Child (*Homo habilis*)	1960	Louis and Jonathan Leakey	Olduvai Gorge	The first example of this species ever found. Fragments of the skull were actually found before "Zinj" but were not identified until later. Several other skulls were found nearby and were given names such as George and Twiggy. Stone flakes found at the site suggest that H. habilis was the first to make use of stone tools.

KNM-ER 1470 (*Homo habilis*)	1972	Bernard Ngeneo and Richard Leakey	Lake Turkana	This 2- to 3-million-year-old skull with a large brain was Richard Leakey's first discovery of major importance. Because it was the same age as *A. boisei*, it provided the first evidence that the *Homo* line did not evolve from the more ape-like australopithecines.
Footprints (unknown)	1978	Mary Leakey	Laetoli	This long trail of footprints of three individuals proved that human ancestors were walking upright as early as 3.6 million years ago. From the stride length, they were small, only about 4 feet, 6 inches tall. Fossil bones were found in the same layer of rock. Some scientists say that the creatures were *A. afarensis*; others call them *A. africanus*; still others say they are not australopithecines but something else which led to the *Homo* line.
Turkana Boy	1984	Kamoya Kimeu and Richard Leakey	Lake Turkana	This nearly complete skeleton constitutes the earliest set of one individual's bones ever found, dated at 1.6 million years. The individual was about twelve years old when he died and stood about 5 feet, 4 inches tall. As an adult, he may have reached 6 feet, contradicting earlier thoughts that human ancestors were tiny.

Glossary

Anthropology: The study of human beings, especially their culture and habits.

Archaeology: The study of fossils, tools, monuments, and art left behind by human and prehuman cultures.

Artifact: Any object whose shape or existence is not caused by natural forces. Examples include flints made by hominid ancestors.

Australopithecus: A genus of hominid, more primitive than *Homo*. *Zinjanthropus* belongs to this genus.

Cast: A reproduction of an object like a fossil, created by coating the fossil with plaster or foam and then allowing the material to harden. Sometimes a natural cast may form, as when mud fills a skull.

Fossils: The bones or impressions of creatures that were once alive. Fossils are usually found embedded in rock that was once mud or volcanic ash.

Genus (*plural*, genera): One of the groups in the system of scientific names that classifies all living things. Members of a genus are more closely related than members of different "families" (another classification) but not as closely related as members of the same species.

Hominid: Any member of the family Hominidae. This includes *Homo* and *Australopithecus*, but not the apes.

Homo: The genus name of humans and their closest relatives, often abbreviated in species names as *H*. Recognized species include *H. sapiens*, *H. erectus*, and *H. habilis*.

Paleoanthropology: The study of hominids. It usually involves the search for and study of fossils and tools.

Potassium-argon dating: A method of determining the age of volcanic rocks and tuff. It is based on the rate of decay of a radioactive form of potassium.

Proconsul: A prehominid genus that lived around 18 million years ago in Africa. *Proconsul* was a quadruped; that is, it walked on four feet. It may have been an ancestor to all modern apes.

Ramapithecus: A genus of ape-like creatures that lived in Africa 14 million years ago. *Ramapithecus* was once thought to be the most recent ancestor to humans and apes.

Stone Age: The period of time, beginning about 2 million years ago, when human ancestors were making and using stone tools. The Stone Age is divided into three periods: Paleolithic, Mesolithic, and Neolithic.

Tuff: Volcanic ash that has clumped. Traces of tuff at research sites can be used to determine the age of each site.

Zinjanthropus: The former genus name of the species *Australopithecus boisei*, originally thought by Louis Leakey to be a separate genus. The name means "man of East Africa."

Bibliography

Cole, Sonia. *Leakey's Luck*. New York: Harcourt Brace Jovanovich, 1975. The major biography of Louis Leakey, written by a friend of the family with the family's help. The book covers both Leakey's work and his private life. It is a fairly balanced account, presenting both positive and negative aspects of Louis Leakey's character. Some readers may find the lengthy family history and personal activities somewhat dull.

Johanson, Donald, and Maitland Edey. *Lucy: The Beginnings of Humankind*. New York: Simon & Schuster, 1981. Johanson's personal account of the discovery of one of the most famous hominid fossils. Johanson also gives his version of the problems between him and the Leakey family over the years. The book is well illustrated, easy to read, and very entertaining. Johanson also co-authored another book, *Lucy's Child: The Discovery of a Human Ancestor* (New York: William Morrow, 1989), which continues the story begun in *Lucy*.

Kevles, Bettyann. *Watching the Great Apes: The Primate Studies of Goodall, Fossey, and Galdikas*. New York: E. P. Dutton, 1976. Written for general readers and young adults, this volume presents a clear summary of the work of Louis Leakey's three "primate protégés." Three of the chapters are fictional accounts of the lives of the great apes. The book includes a bibliography and a chart comparing the characteristics of chimpanzees, gorillas, and orangutans.

Leakey, L. S. B. *By the Evidence: Memoirs, 1932-1951*. New York: Harcourt Brace Jovanovich, 1974. Leakey's second autobiography, written shortly before his death. Like *White African*, the book contains mostly personal anecdotes.

_____. *White African: An Early Autobiography*. Cambridge, Mass.: Schenkman, 1937. Covers the early years of Louis Leakey's life. Very little space is devoted to archaeology; this is mostly a story of a young man growing up in colonial Africa.

Leakey, Mary. *Africa's Vanishing Art*. New York: Doubleday, 1983. For those interested in ancient art, this book features tracings of prehistoric cave paintings studied by the Leakeys. Mary provides commentary on the art and its possible meaning and purpose.

_____. *Disclosing the Past*. Garden City, N.Y.: Doubleday, 1984. Mary's autobiography. Unlike Louis, Mary devotes much more discussion to her work, especially to the events leading up to important discoveries. The style is very personal, as if the reader and author were having a private chat.

Leakey, Richard. *One Life: An Autobiography*. London: Michael Joseph, 1983. Following in the footsteps of his parents, Richard wrote his own autobiography. This book covers the time up to his kidney transplant. Offers much interesting information and engaging anecdotes: Richard's account of using camels on an expedition is especially amusing. The book is well illustrated with photographs and drawings.

Leakey, Richard, and Roger Lewin. *Origins: What New Discoveries Reveal About the Emergence of Our Species and Its Possible Future*. New York: E. P. Dutton, 1977. This work is especially interesting for what it reveals about Richard's theories and philosophies. The authors address such questions as "How did intelligence and language develop?" and "Are humans naturally aggressive?" Photographs and illustrations appear on nearly every page.

_____. *Origins Reconsidered: In Search of What Makes Us Human*. New York: Doubleday, 1992. This book is a continuation of Leakey and Lewin's popular first book. It is divided into six parts, each of which focuses on a different definition of "human." The first section is devoted to archaeology and concentrates on Leakey's discovery of the *Homo erectus* skeleton called Turkana Boy.

Lewin, Roger. *Bones of Contention: Controversies in the Search for Human Origins*. New York: Simon & Schuster, 1987. The text reads like a thriller or a mystery story. Each chapter is devoted to a different controversy. Louis, Mary, and Richard are prominently featured.

_____. *Human Evolution: An Illustrated Introduction*. New York: W. H. Freeman, 1984. A wonderful book, filled with pictures, maps, and illustrations on nearly every page. Some of the material is fairly sophisticated, but the graphics alone make this large-size paperback well worth finding.

Parker, Steve. *The Practical Paleontologist*. New York: Simon & Schuster, 1990. A very interesting volume for someone inspired by the Leakeys, who wants to find fossils. Includes a history of paleontology, lists of important museums and parks to visit, and information on finding, preserving, and identifying fossils.

Weaver, Kenneth F. "The Search for Our Ancestors." *National Geographic* 168, no. 5 (1985): 560-623. This article reviews the history behind the search for hominids. The cover of the issue features the holographic image of a hominid skull. The article also has a fold-out section with an artist's illustrations of what the different hominids may have looked like. It is immediately followed by an article by Richard Leakey and Alan Walker which covers the discovery of a skull of a twelve-year-old boy identified as *Homo erectus*.

Media Resources

British Broadcasting Corporation, producers. *The Making of Mankind.*
Video, 7 parts, each 52 minutes. 1981. Distributed by Pennsylvania State
University Audio-Visual Services. This seven-part series, narrated by
Richard Leakey, examines fossil evidence from the earliest hominids and
its implications for human evolution. Part 2, "One Small Step . . . ,"
features Mary Leakey's discovery of the Laetoli footprints.

Crimmons, James C., producer. *Evidence.* Video, 18 minutes. 1977.
Distributed by Karol Media. Available for rent from Washington State
University Audio Visual Services. This video is part of a series called
The Search for Solutions. Narrated by Stacy Keach, it includes many
different types of evidence, and how information can be used to prove or
disprove theories. Part of the video, subtitled "Man at the Beginning,"
reviews the anthropological evidence unearthed by Richard Leakey.

Goldmark Associates, producers. *Richard Leakey: Looking Ahead to the
Past.* Video, 35 minutes. 1988. Distributed by Carolina Biological
Supply Company. This video is part of Carolina's The Eminent
Scientists series and was created for high school audiences. Also
included in this series is a 30-minute video of the work of Jane Goodall,
entitled *A Life in the Wild.*

Kane, Dennis, and Thomas Skinner, producers. *The Legacy of L. S. B.
Leakey.* Video and 16mm film, 57 minutes. 1989. Distributed by Karol
Media. This documentary on Louis Leakey's life and career was
broadcast originally as a National Geographic television special.

National Geographic Society, producers. *Dr. Leakey and the Dawn of Man.*
16mm film, 28 minutes. 1967. Distributed by Films Incorporated and
Karol Media. This film, an edited version of a National Geographic
television special which first aired on November 5, 1966, includes a
review of Louis Leakey's life and work.

National Geographic Society, producers. *Leakey.* Video and 16 mm film, 22
minutes. 1983. Available for rental from Karol Media and the
Pennsylvania State University Audio-Visual Services. This educational
film is available with a teacher's guide. It is a biography of Louis
Leakey, beginning with his childhood in Africa. Also included is
information on the work of Mary and Richard Leakey and interviews
with Jane Goodall, Dian Fossey, and Biruté Galdikas.

National Geographic Society and WQED, producers. *Mysteries of Mankind.*

PIONEERS

Video, 60 minutes. 1988. Distributed by the National Geographic Society and Carolina Biological Supply Company. This video presents an overview of the physical and molecular evidence on human origins. It features the discoveries of the Leakey family, Donald Johanson, and more recent work of molecular biologists.

INDEX

Animal Kingdom, 24
Apes, 90
Australopithecus, 25
Australopithecus afarensis, 22, 66
Australopithecus boisei, 22, 42, 75
Avern, Frida, 28-29

Behrensmeyer, Kay, 82-83
Bipedalism, 65
Brooks, Alison, 93

Calico Hills conference, 47
Cambridge University, 14-15, 18
Carter, Howard, 29
Chimpanzees, 87-88
Clark, William Le Gros, 38, 44
Coryndon Museum. *See* Kenya
    National Museum.
Cropper, Margaret. *See* Leakey,
    Margaret.
Cutler, W. E., 15, 16

Dart, Raymond, 44
Dating techniques, 76, 82, 93
Disclosing the Past, 31, 69
DNA sequences, 95

Epps, Meave. *See* Leakey, Meave.

Fossey, Dian, 88-90
Fossils, defined, 21
Foundation for Research into the
    Origins of Man (FROM), 96

Galdikas, Biruté, 90
Goodall, Jane, 87-88
Gorillas, 88-90
Gorillas in the Mist, 90
Grant, Nellie, 34

Hadar (Afar Triangle), 66, 91
Haile Selassie, 78
Hollywood, 39
Hominid Gang, 46-47, 83
Hominids, defined, 22, 24-25
Homo erectus, 22, 24, 85
Homo habilis, 22, 24, 42-45, 71, 83
Homo sapiens, 22, 24
Human beings, classification of,
    21-25
Hyrax Hill, 34

Johanson, Donald, 66, 67, 91-93
"Jonny's Child." See *Homo habilis*.

Katanda, 93
Kenya, 11, 33
Kenya National Museum, 35, 81
Kenyatta, Jomo, 32-33, 78
Kikuyu people, 11, 33, 34
Kimeu, Kamoya, 47, 75, 79, 85
King Solomon's Mines, 39
Koinange, Chief, 11, 34
Koobi Foora, 82-86

Laetoli, Tanzania, discovery of
    hominid footprints, 47-48,
    65-66, 92
Lake Turkana. *See* Turkana, Lake.

Leakey, Colin Louis, 29, 70

Leakey, Jonathan, 71-72, 75; birth, 35; discovery of *Homo habilis*, 42

Leakey, Louis Seymour Bazett, birth and youth, 11-12; death of, 83; education, 12-19; marriage to Frida Avern, 29; marriage to Mary Douglas Nicol, 29

Leakey, Margaret, 75

Leakey, Mary, birth and childhood, 29-33; blindness in left eye, 67-69; discovery of hominid footprints at Laetoli, 47-48, 65-66; discovery of *Zinjanthropus boisei*, 41; education, 31-33; Linnaeus Medal, 67; marriage to L. S. B. Leakey, 33

Leakey, Meave, 82, 83

Leakey, Philip, 35, 65, 71, 74

Leakey, Priscilla Muthoni, 29, 70

Leakey, Richard Erskine Frere, 35, 70-77; birth, 35; curatorship of Kenya National Museum, 81-82; early expeditions, 74-75; education, 72; kidney failure, 82; marriage to Margaret Cropper, 75; marriage to Meave Epps, 83

Lemozi, Abbé, 29-31

Liddell, Dorothy, 31

Lothagam Hill, 85

Loveridge, Arthur, 12

L. S. B. Leakey Foundation for Research Related to Man's Origin, 95

Lucy, 91-93

Lucy: The Beginnings of Mankind, 91

Mau Mau rebellion, 33

Miocene era, 36

Molecular biology, 93-95

National Geographic Society, 42, 48, 74-75, 79, 81

Neanderthals, 79

Newsom, Bernard H., 28

Ngeneo, Bernard, 83, 85

Nicol, Mary Douglas. *See* Leakey, Mary.

Nutcracker Man. See *Zinjanthropus boisei*.

Olduvai Gorge, 28, 38-45, 74

Olorgesailie, 35

Omo Valley, 78-79, 86

Paleoanthropology, defined, 20

Piltdown hoax, 21

Potassium-argon (dating technique), 82

Primatology, 87

Proconsul africanus, 22, 25, 36-38

Ramapithecus, 25

Reck, Hans, 39

Rusinga Island, 36

St. John's College, 14-15

Sarich, Vincent, 95

Sivapithecus, 25

Skull 1470, 83-85, 94

String figures, 17-18

Tanganyika, 15

Tanzania, 15

Thermoluminescence (dating technique), 76, 93
Tieb, Maurice, 91
"Tuff," 82
Turkana, Lake, 78-86
Turkana Boy, 85

Weymouth College, 12-14
White, Tim, 48, 65, 67
Wilson, Allan, 95

Yellen, John, 93

Zinjanthropus boisei, 22, 30, 40-42, 89